PRAISE FOR
REWRITE YOUR FINANCIAL NARRATIVE

In Rewrite Your Financial Narrative, *Fred Wollman uses insights gained through a lifetime of education and personal experience to clearly explain, in client-friendly terms, his approach to financial health and wellbeing. I feel he has made the complicated, confusing, and often contradictory world of personal financial planning easy to understand, implement, and maintain. I see this as a must read for clients to gently coach them on how to think about their personal finances and future.*

Larry Divers, CISP®, CRA®, CRC®, CRSP™, AIFA®, AIFM™

Executive Vice President, Cannon Financial Institute

"His concept of a financial GPS to calculate and then recalculate the best route through the maze of financial options is presented in a fresh, even humorous manner and I found it to be an easy read."

Linda Schwader

Speaker, author, and business coach

"Fred Wollman's down-to-earth advice and focus on each client's personal situation makes clear through anecdotes and easy-to-understand illustrations how each of us can benefit in setting our GPS to reach our goals. I think this book will benefit both clients and advisors who take the time to read it and follow the common-sense advice Fred imparts from his long experience as a financial advisor."

Terry Prendergast, JD

Frequent lecturer on South Dakota dynasty, directed, community property, and asset protection trusts

"Fred's book is refreshing to me in its transparency and personal approach. Instead of telling the audience what to do and how to make the perfect decision, he empathizes with them regarding the financial challenges we all face because we have all been there."

Edward J. Bosch, Jr., LUTCF, AIF®

Accredited Investment Fiduciary Designee®

"Upon reading this I thought, finally, something written in plain English for people who are really not interested in financial topics but know they should know more."

Brooke Kelley

Business coach and author, Kelley Group International

rewrite

~~write~~

your

financial

narrative

~~write~~ rewrite
your
financial
narrative

Eliminate Retirement Guesswork by Managing Risk,
Minimizing Income Tax, and Building a More
Predictable Income Stream

fred wollman, CFP® MPAS®

Published by Advantage, Charleston, South Carolina.
Member of Advantage Media Group.

ADVANTAGE is a registered trademark, and the Advantage colophon is a trademark of Advantage Media Group, Inc.

Printed in the United States of America.

10 9 8 7 6 5 4 3 2 1

ISBN: 978-1-59932-857-7
LCCN: 2017961320

Cover design by Katie Biondo.
Layout design by Megan Elger.

Advantage Media Group is proud to be a part of the Tree Neutral® program. Tree Neutral offsets the number of trees consumed in the production and printing of this book by taking proactive steps such as planting trees in direct proportion to the number of trees used to print books. To learn more about Tree Neutral, please visit **www.treeneutral.com.**

Advantage Media Group is a publisher of business, self-improvement, and professional development books. We help entrepreneurs, business leaders, and professionals share their Stories, Passion, and Knowledge to help others Learn & Grow. Do you have a manuscript or book idea that you would like us to consider for publishing? Please visit advantagefamily.com or call **1.866.775.1696.**

Table of Contents

Introduction 1

Chapter 1 3

**A Careful Look in the Mirror:
Assessing Dreams and Motivations**

Chapter 2 15

**Activating Your Financial GPS:
Identify Your Financial Reality**

Chapter 3 31

**Guidelines to Understanding Money:
Risk, Volatility and Portfolio Building**

Chapter 4 49

**Economic Potholes and Pitfalls: How to
Avoid—and Conquer—Financial Biases**

Chapter 5 61

**The Four Greatest Risks to
Your Financial Health**

Chapter 6 75

**A Fork in the Road: A Guide for
Pre-Retirement Investors**

Chapter 7 85

**The Time Is Now: Financial Strategies
for the Retirement Years**

Chapter 8 101

**What's Yours Is Yours:
Protecting Your Assets**

Chapter 9 109

**Passing on the Wealth: "Who's
Gonna Get the Money, Honey?"**

Resources 127

Contact 129

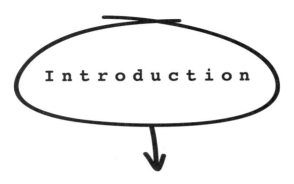

Introduction

I should begin with a not-so-subtle disclaimer. If you're looking for a book that's going to outline a "can't-miss" get-rich-quick scheme, you've picked up the wrong bundle of paper. This book is not a tutorial on how to maximize the return on your investment, nor is it designed to eliminate downside risk in your investment portfolio. If you're looking for any of the above, save yourself some time and go rummaging through a different bookshelf.

This is a book that's been written for real people who live real lives—people who have real families and real dreams, and those who recognize that life will inevitably be filled with grand moments and tragic disappointments. It's a book for realists, written by a realist—with the intent of helping honest people get their financial lives in focus and develop a game plan to deal with all of the speed bumps that life will inevitably throw their way.

Why did I write this book? Because, after being in this industry since 1980, I've found that far too many people go to financial advisors looking for comfortable answers to all the wrong questions.

Too often financial planners focus exclusively on selling products. It's all about rates of return or avoiding the next financial crisis because (a) the client doesn't know enough about finances to focus on anything else, or (b) the advisor may have his or her own personal agenda.

It's my opinion, however, that most people need to think more about their goals, their priorities, what they want to accomplish, and what's *really* important to them.

Whenever I sit down with potential clients, I always ask them what they hope to gain from their relationship with a financial advisor. In a perfect world, what do you want a financial advisor to do for you? What are your expectations? What are you trying to accomplish? Ideally, what would your relationship with your advisor look like?

People often tend to focus far too intensely on single pieces of the puzzle as opposed to the whole picture. That is why this book has been designed to help people make good financial decisions and aid them in understanding how and why they've come to think about money the way they do.

Who should read this book? Plain and simple: people who have a desire to gain a firm grip on their financial affairs. As well as people who are tired of—or worried about—how their financial affairs might play out moving forward.

Let's face it, we're all sprinting through life at a hundred miles an hour. We've all got relationships, jobs, families, and then one day it happens: you have that OMG moment. "Am I going to have enough money to be able to stop working someday? Do I have enough to stop working now? How much do I need to save? When will I have enough money to stop working?"

Anyone who wants to know the answers to these questions should flip the page and read on. The path forward lies in the pages that follow.

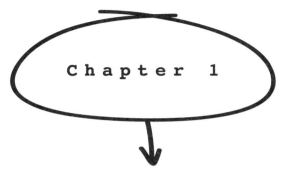

A Careful Look in the Mirror: Assessing Dreams and Motivations

"A goal without a plan is just a wish."
—Antoine de Saint-Exupéry

Whenever I sit down with a client for the first time, I always begin by posing a deceptively difficult question: "If you had unlimited money, how would you spend it?"

At first glance, it seems like a pretty easy question to answer, doesn't it? To put it another way: "Ideally, what do you want the rest of your life to look like? What do you really want out of life?"

Initially, I tend to get some pretty standard answers. People often tell me they want to make sure they have enough money to live independently, so they don't become a burden to their children. Others offer a wish list including travel, paying for weddings, educating the kids or grandkids, or a catalogue of things they never got around to doing while they were working or taking care of the kids.

If I've learned anything over the years, it's that those initial responses don't really tell the whole story. It's only when I ask my follow-up question—"*Why* do you want to do those things?"—that we begin to get to the root of the matter.

If people tell me that they don't want to be a burden to their children, my next question will often be, "*Why?*" *Why* is that the first thing they chose to say? Is it because their grandparents ended up living with their parents? Are they afraid their parents are going to end up living with them?

In my opinion, not enough financial advisors bother to delve into these crucially important *why* questions. I fundamentally believe that the motivations fueling our individual goals are often more important than the content of the goals themselves. *Why?* Because these questions help unveil the underlying emotions behind our decisions. Ultimately, when it comes to financial matters, emotions often drive our actions. Your job. Family stress. Market fluctuations. All these apply pressure in unpredictable ways. Sometimes such pressure is a good thing and can lead to positive changes. However, sometimes it is an unwanted force which can cause costly mistakes.

I fundamentally believe that the motivations fueling our individual goals are often more important than the content of the goals themselves.

As much as we like to think we're logical, rational human beings, in most cases we end up making decisions based on what we're feeling at a particular point in time. Thus, it's incredibly important for financial advisors, like myself, to know where our clients' emotional triggers lie. In doing so, we can understand why particular decisions have been made and then redirect them toward a more rational choice.

These questions are also important because they allow us to talk about the difference between goals and priorities. Goals are milestones or accomplishments: things you can check off a list. A priority is very different. A priority is something that needs to happen no matter what … and sometimes at the expense of everything else.

I've discovered that asking these questions early in the discussion helps ground the conversations that follow. Oftentimes, my clients may initially believe something is really important to them. However, after all the goals are listed and the client is asked, "What's most important to *you*? Why is that important?" people sometimes make different decisions.

Once we find our way to that point—that essential truth about what they desire—we're starting from the right place. We've set a destination, the place where we need to go. Once we've plotted that point on the map, we can start charting the most effective course to get there.

THE FIVE PILLARS OF FINANCIAL PLANNING

To get to where you want to go in retirement, it's critical that you do two things: (1) determine where you want to go (the fun part), as well as (2) figure out where you are currently (the more challenging part). This is why, during the early discussions, I'm committed to learning five things about each of my clients.

1. **What is your current situation in life?** How old are you? What's your income? How much are you saving? What assets have you accumulated?

2. **What are your financial and lifestyle goals?** I break them down into needs, wants, and wishes. Here's how I define them in simple terms:

- **Needs** are things you require; you must pay them to live your life the way you live it. Think electricity bills, groceries, health insurance. When the roof starts leaking, you have to fix it.

- **Wants** are things you'd like to do and would be disappointed if you didn't do at some point in your life. You could live without them, but not without feeling at least a little regret. These are things like going on yearly vacations, buying a new car periodically, or paying for your child's wedding.

- **Wishes** are the sort of things that happen if everything goes just right, like that new Corvette you've been dreaming about, or your long-planned but yet-to-be realized six-month trip around the world. A second home in Maui. These are all things you would like to have or experience, but you would be okay if they didn't materialize.

3. **What are your priorities?** What is most important to you now (i.e., the next two, three, or five years) and in the longer term—down the road? What priorities need to happen "no matter what"? What will you sacrifice to make them happen?

4. **What do you want your future to look like?** How do you want your life to be when you're not going to your job every day? What's going to occupy your time? Are you going to be babysitting grandkids every day? Are you going to be taking world cruises? Are you going to be working thirty hours a week as a volunteer in your community?

5. **What are your family dynamics?**

- How old are your children? What are they like? Will any of them never leave home?

- Which ones do you expect will go to college? Graduate school? Never get a job?

- Who has a substance abuse problem?

- Are there any behavioral issues with the kids, their spouses, or the grandchildren?

- Are your parents still living? If so, do you anticipate the need or possibility of supporting them either physically (maybe allowing them to move in with you some day) or financially?

- What is the possibility of this occurring? Will it be in the near term or is that a long time in the future?

- Are there other family members—perhaps aunts, uncles, nieces—who may impact your life?

Knowing this information will help us create a viable long-term financial plan for you and your family.

On the surface, most financial plans are drawn up like plug-and-play software programs. They are nothing more than cold algorithms because they're based solely on numbers. "If I'm this old, I need to have this much money, and if my risk tolerance is this, then this is how my money needs to be invested. If I've got this much money, this is how much money I can afford to spend during my retirement because that's what the numbers say."

However, if your financial advisor fully understands your priorities, then he or she can provide you with ideas, suggestions, and alternatives on how you can achieve your dreams. At some point, it stops being just about the numbers. Your "why" becomes your plan.

In truth, the uniqueness of the client and their particular situations is what should dictate priorities. That's why, in my opinion, there's no such thing as a one-size-fits-all financial plan. Everybody's situation is unique, as is every single financial plan I write for my individual clients.

LESSONS FROM THE PAST

Early in my career, I would come into meetings with new clients, collect some preliminary numbers, and then present my agenda for what should happen. I had already decided what needed to happen before I got there. It was *my* plan for them. Financial plans—as I've since learned all too well—can only be tailored to meet an individual's distinctive needs after you take the time to listen to that individual and discover the truth about his or her situation.

Robert Shiller, a professor of economics at Yale, and one of the most influential economists in the United States, wrote a paper about the concept of "narrative economics." His paper laments that people in the economics field, to their detriment, have never paid as much attention to narratives as writers and journalists.

Schiller thinks that's a mistake, in part because economists always deem narratives and stories to be patently unscientific. That's true. Stories are not scientific, but that doesn't mean they're not powerful. We communicate with narratives, catalogue our memories through them, and are often motivated by the desire to be a part of grand narratives ourselves.

There's no doubt about it: The narrative you've got running through your head, no matter what it's about, is going to influence how you act. It's telling you what you should be doing. To be effective, a financial planner needs to understand the narratives that are motivating their client's financial decisions.

THE BEACH HOUSE THAT NEVER WAS

Since I believe in the importance of my clients sharing their financial narratives, I think it's important to share a portion of my own narrative—one that leads to what I believe is a very important lesson.

Early in my career, when I was studying for my CFP° certification, I had to write my own financial plan for my family. At the time, my goal was as straightforward as it was simple: I wanted to be able to retire at fifty-five with a house on the beach. I was in my early thirties, and fifty-five seemed like a long way off, so a house on the beach sounded like a good idea.

I crunched the numbers and found, to my dismay, the chance of my wife and I reaching our goal was slim unless we redefined our "beach house" as a cardboard box tucked under a pier in Oceanside, California. There just wasn't enough going on in our lives at the time, financially speaking, to save enough money to accomplish our goal.

Fast forward to when my eldest daughter was about twelve, and I realized once again that I hadn't saved a whole lot of money for her education. I thought, "Okay, Fred. Here's the deal. If you can save as much as you can over the next four to six years for her college— knowing that her brother was just four years behind her—you might be able to, if you're lucky, start saving for retirement at age fifty-two."

I said to myself, "There is another choice." The decision my wife and I made at that time was to say, "Let the kids wait." We decided to save like crazy for our retirement until they started college, and if we had to stop saving for retirement and pay for their education out of cash flow, at least we would have the amount of money saved prior to them starting school. When our first grandchild was born, we repeated our discussion and determined again to not specifically set aside money for him.

My first responsibility was, and still is, to make sure that my wife and I are financially solvent. Anything above and beyond our own solvency is a different story. The unconventional lesson of my little parable? *Put yourself first when it comes to your finances. Then you can take care of others with your excess funds.* It is just like the oxygen mask on an airplane. Put your mask on first, and then take care of the child in the next seat. There is a reason we are told to perform those tasks in that sequence.

THE PHASES OF LIFE

The old maxim is true. Life does go by in a blink. Think about it for a moment. Although everyone has a different narrative, our lives tend to fall into certain clearly defined phases.

- student

- in a relationship and working

- raising a family

- paying for college/paying for weddings/parents moving in with you

- seriously thinking about retirement: "pre-retirement"

- retired

- planning your legacy

All these phases of life have to be dealt with in different ways—mentally, emotionally, and financially. As a student, you need beer money and a date for the weekend. With a young family, it's all about good schools, a nice neighborhood, and paying the bills—all the while wondering if you're saving enough money for retirement.

This is supposed to be the accumulation phase. You know you should be saving money—but you know you are not saving enough. Life just keeps getting in the way of saving money. Kids need new shoes. They are playing sports. The car breaks down. The roof leaks. Somebody wants to go to private school versus public school. I "need" a vacation. Thus, savings plans get initiated but are rarely fully executed, as it becomes difficult to accumulate enough in the face of all these recurring demands on your finances.

Then comes the "time to catch up and get-it-done" phase—what I call the pre-retirement phase—which is that point in life where the kids are out of college and hopefully not living in the basement. You are experiencing your peak earning years, and it's still a long while before you turn in your resignation. These are the make-it-or-break-it years. I'll give more details on this in chapter 6.

A dear friend of mine made a comment one day that I'll never forget. He said he never saved any money until he was fifty years old. But, in the end, he found a way to make up for lost time. So have faith and create a plan.

If you're looking at retirement in your mid-sixties, you likely have 30 percent of your life still in front of you. According to the Social Security Administration, a man aged sixty-five will live to age eighty-four, and the average woman to age eighty-seven. One in four sixty-five-year-olds will live past ninety and one in ten past age ninety-five. If you start talking about couples, there is a 75 percent chance one person lives to age eighty-five, a 50 percent chance that one person lives to ninety, and a 25 percent chance that someone lives to ninety-five.

The question is, what are you going to do with yourself? What are you going to do with your time? Have you sat down and really thought about how much money it's going to take to get you there? Do you have any financial constraints that might prevent you from doing all the things you think you may want to do? Financial constraints aren't necessarily bad things, but you have to recognize what those constraints might be, come to terms with them, and make adjustments.

Remember, there will be one more phase in your life, which I call the **legacy phase**.

The legacy phase is that point in life where your doctors have all started to retire or maybe have already retired, and the new doctor looks like he or she should still be in high school or, at the very latest, going to spring break in Miami. More on this in chapter 8.

DEGREES OF FREEDOM

Financial planning is all about helping people discover their "Personal Degree of Freedom." The answer lies in your own personal narrative. What do you need? What do you require to feel secure—to get to that place where you believe things are going to be okay? What does it take to make you feel comfortable so a panic attack doesn't hit when you run into one of life's many speed bumps?

The roof needs to be repaired. The vehicle needs a fix. One of your adult children comes to you and says, "I've lost my job." What do you require to feel comfortable enough to know you can weather these storms physically, mentally, emotionally, and financially? If the stock market plummets 30 percent next month, what do you need to prevent yourself from panicking and anticipating living on a park bench for the rest of your life?

What do you need to develop a sense of freedom or the belief that you can handle all the obstacles that life might present you? Because, let's be honest, we're all going to encounter plenty of challenges down the ever-winding road of life.

Financial advisors aren't paid to be your shrink. The good ones, however, can help you understand what these events really mean, financially speaking, as opposed to what you think they mean based on your own personal narrative. In other words, is the narrative running in your head based upon reality?

The clients outline their desired destination. My job is to chart a course. I offer alternative routes for you to reach your goal. You make some decisions. Then, six months or a year later, we look at where you are relative to your objectives and say, "Are we working in that direction, or are we off-course?" If we're off-course, what do we do to return to the path we want to travel?

Life is full of challenges and opportunities. You want to be able to deal with those challenges and take advantage of unforeseen opportunities when they arise. You should be flexible, keep your eyes open, and be willing to make course corrections. You never know what's around the next corner.

I tell people that most financial plans are extremely accurate and very applicable—until they leave my parking lot. Once they're off the property, life happens. Things change. This is not a one-and-done, static process. This is a process of ebb and flow.

Sometimes you can see obstacles coming a mile away, while at other times surprises jump up and slap you in the face. The idea is to be flexible and realize this is an ongoing, dynamic process that never really ends. Let's begin …

"One's destination is never a place,
but a new way of seeing things."

—Henry Miller

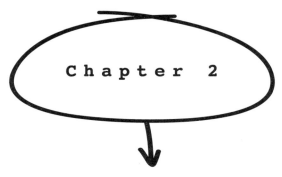

Activating Your Financial GPS: Identify Your Financial Reality

"It ain't what you know that gets you in trouble. It's that what you know that just ain't true is what gets you in trouble."

—Mark Twain

Every single client who has ever walked into my office—without exception—has always come equipped with what I call a financial narrative. These are the stories we tell ourselves to explain why we're in the financial situation we're in. These stories—some true, some pure fiction—are often recycled in our minds until they become our perceived reality.

By this point in my career, I've heard countless financial narratives, most of which include variations on the same themes:

- **The Pessimist:** "I'm never going to be able to retire; I'm going to have to work forever."

- **The Optimist:** "Between my Social Security and my pension, I have enough money coming in to cover the bills I currently have, so that must mean I have enough to retire."

- **The Short-Sighted**: "I have lots of money. I have a tremendous net worth, so money is never going to be a concern."

- **The Gamblers**: "I've done a great job of picking stocks over the last eight years, so I should always be able to do a great job picking stocks. I can retire now and live on the profits from my investments just based on picking stocks."

- **The Windfallers**: "I inherited a bunch of wealth. I'm rich. I can buy whatever I want and never have a money worry for the rest of my life."

Sometimes these financial narratives are very accurate. But, in most cases, the stories we tell ourselves aren't rooted in any type of reality whatsoever. They're fairy tales. Whether these narratives are too optimistic or too pessimistic doesn't matter. The truth is, clients who hold onto a false sense of reality are doing themselves a disservice. It's like the movie *La La Land*. If you don't know what's real and what's imaginary, you're destined to meet disappointments somewhere along the line.

This is why I see it as one of my principle responsibilities to (a) help people form an accurate picture of their financial reality, and (b) help them see if their narrative syncs with their reality.

NAVIGATING YOUR FINANCIAL GPS

When my clients and I sit down to discuss their financial narrative, what we're really doing is calibrating and programing what I refer to as their "financial GPS." It's similar to the GPS systems we use in our phones or cars, but this one is for the financial journey.

Think about your typical GPS for a moment. The first thing you do is program where you want to go, right? This becomes the first "blue dot." In terms of your finances, that involves laying out your retirement goals and priorities, which we discussed in chapter 1.

After you type in the address of your destination on a traditional GPS, the device will ask you another question: "What is your current location?" or "Would you like to use your current location?" If you answer yes, a second blue dot shows up on the map.

That's what we're doing in this part of the financial-planning process. We're figuring out exactly where you are today. Without that, you can't determine the best route moving forward.

To do so, it's important to ask yourself a series of questions. The list is too long to print in full here, but here's a sampling of what you can expect to cover in our early discussions:

- How many years do you have until you want to retire?

- How much do you currently have in investments, including your 401(k), money in the bank, brokerage accounts, other retirement savings, and outside investments in things like real estate?

- How much debt do you have? Do you have a plan to retire this debt?

- How much money do you spend now?

- Will you want to change your place of residence someday?

- Are there major items you would like to spend money on after retiring?

- What are your family dynamics?

The only major number worth excluding in this discussion is the equity you've accumulated in your home. Why? Because if you sell that house, there's a high likelihood that you'll take that equity and drop it into the next property. The only time it's prudent to include the equity in a home is when someone says, "I'm going to sell my house and move to a place where housing is far less expensive, and I'll have a bunch of freed-up capital from the sale of my house." Aside from that circumstance, don't include the house.

By gathering this information, we can ascertain your current financial situation. Good, bad, ugly—it doesn't matter. It's just a point on the map, but we absolutely must identify that point before we can start moving forward.

At this point, a person's narrative often begins to change. The narrative stops being fiction and becomes a true story. If the story we uncover for you is a promising one, congratulations. You've done a great job. You've worked hard, saved hard, and have probably been kind of lucky. Good work.

On the other hand, if that situation is not so pretty—heck, it might even be downright ugly—you're already in better shape than when we started the process because you know where you are. Congratulations on discovering your starting point.

This is a critical step for clients with a spouse who might not be as keyed into their finances or have a very different perception of reality compared to their partner. If the spouse has a totally different narrative running through his or her head, now both of them can see where they are on the map. That's a critical starting point in getting both parties to work together toward a mutually agreeable plan. If they're going to get to where they both want to go, they have to start from the same place.

THE FINANCIAL IMPORTANCE OF MEMORIES

Most people's financial narratives were formed a long time ago. They may not have given any conscious thought as to how those stories took shape until they sit down and talk about them. Which is why I always ask my clients what some might consider an odd question: "Tell me your first recollection of money or your first memory of money as a child."

I ask this because our attitudes and philosophies regarding money are developed very, very early in our lives, often from the people we grew up with: the parents, relatives, and mentors who were meaningful to us in our lives. These early interactions truly do shape who we become as adults, and ultimately become valuable in helping us map out a plan for future success.

I remember, for example, one of my clients telling me how, as a third-grader, he used to take his twenty-five-cent allowance to elementary school to buy US savings stamps. He talked in glowing terms about how he would fill this little book with twenty-five-cent stamps. When it was completely stamped over, the book could be returned to get a twenty-five dollar savings bond. He did that for many, many years, and later used the money to pay for college.

Another person told me that he and a buddy, when they were about twelve years old, had a popcorn stand. They would operate this popcorn stand on Saturday nights in the downtown area of a small town in the Midwest. They'd make money by selling popcorn to the farmers when they came into town to buy groceries.

Another client told me her first recollection of money was from middle school. Her family had been evicted from their apartment. She remembered sitting out on the curb, surrounded by all her family's household possessions, and how embarrassed she felt.

It's undeniable that such experiences have an impact on our lives. Having heard the broad outlines of those stories, try to take a guess as to which person became a saver versus those who became spenders? Which person do you think was the one always filled with financial fear? Which one grew up to be the entrepreneur?

Our memories pertaining to money play a major role in how we perceive money in the present. Everyone should ask themselves something: Is your personal narrative healthy? Does your narrative help you improve your situation? Or is it harmful and poisonous? Is it an obstruction to helping your happiness or in reaching your financial goals?

The beauty of this process is that there are no golden guidelines, no set-in-stone "right ways" or "wrong ways" to invest. Yes, some methods are preferred and increase your odds of success (more on this later). There's no horrible situation that can't be reversed, or any great situation that can't come tumbling down. The whole point of our early work together is to bring about an awareness regarding your situation, your narrative, and your reality, so that you can respond accordingly.

There's no point in beating yourself up for not saving enough money up to this point, nor is it good to have a bad attitude or bad narrative about your current situation. That's not productive. The goal is to identify where you are now, be aware of it, and then move on in a productive way. More often than not, things will improve and get better if you're just *aware* of your financial reality.

If your reality is filled with abundance, you have the opportunity to embrace it during your lifetime as well as share some of it with people, causes, and organizations that are important to you.

IN THE DOOR, OUT THE DOOR: WHAT YOU EARN VERSUS WHAT YOU SPEND

It's important to note that a great many things are simply beyond our control. The whims of the economy, for example, are beyond our control. The jobs we have, to some extent, are beyond our control. And, in many ways, the return we receive on our investments is beyond our control.

In general, there are only two things you have any real control over: (a) how much money you spend, and (b) how much money you save. Beyond that, you can't control much. Life is full of financial ups and downs—exciting good fortune with new jobs or business successes, or crushing defeats with layoffs, illness, or injury, followed by interesting turns, good fortune, and then misfortune. Repeat the cycle.

When I ask new clients about their spending, they often pull out a list of items on it with dollar amounts. That list usually includes things like their mortgage, food, electric and gas bills, and other similar line items with a total at the bottom. This is referred to as the "budget."

One very instructive story involves a good friend of mine who asked me to handle some financial planning for him and his wife. He laid out all his spending in front of me. I looked at his list and gave it to him straight.

"Look," I said. "I've known you a long time. We have to get real here. I know just by looking at this list that these are the numbers you *think* you should be spending—but I doubt this is what you are actually spending. I think you actually spend more." In essence, it was a wish list—what he wanted to be spending every month, as opposed to what he was really spending. That meeting provided me with a very important lesson.

From that point forward, I stopped asking people for their budget. I don't ask my clients how much they plan to spend. I ask them what they are really spending. I want to know what is really going out the door. To do so, they need to look at their bank statement.

The study of monthly bank statements is the beginning of a "basic-needs analysis." In other words, how much money do you need to live in your own home without any extraordinary expenses or travel? Think of it as basic living expenses.

Calculating your basic needs should occur periodically. It's not a one-and-done project. We recalculate this number every year or two when we review and update a client's financial situation. We'll ask clients for three months of bank statements to go through, just to gauge if their spending has changed.

Periodic reviews of expenses are an essential phase of our financial GPS program. We need to identify how far along the path we've gone, where we've been, and when we're estimated to arrive at our destination.

THE SAVINGS GAME

Many people come to us hoping we will hand them a "magic bullet"— the perfect investment plan that will make them guaranteed millionaires. In many people's minds, financial planning and financial success is all about selecting the right investments. They figure that the right investments will inevitably lead to financial freedom. Well, I'm sorry to say that such thinking is flat-out wrong.

Picking the right investments will not necessarily get you where you want to go. The greatest investment in the world is not going to bail you out from inadequate savings. It's saving enough money and collecting enough resources that generates financial freedom.

I suppose, in theory, there are exceptions to this rule. If you're lucky enough to buy the next Apple stock at two bucks a share, then maybe your earnings will offset any inabilities to save money. But frankly, you have the same odds of buying the next Apple at two bucks a share as you have of winning the lottery. So if your financial plan doesn't include buying weekly lottery tickets, then searching for the next super-stock is not the best plan for securing your financial future.

It's saving enough money and collecting enough resources that generates financial freedom.

The best example I can use to illustrate this point involves my parents. Dad was a mailman. Mom was a nurse's aide at the local assisted-living facility. They lived in a nice house, drove nice cars, and liked nice clothes—but they never made a lot of money. Dad died at age eighty-three. Mom passed away at eighty-nine after living in an assisted-living facility for seven years. When my siblings and I sat down to divide their assets, excluding the house, there was $600,000 in their estate.

Mom and Dad were savers, not investors. Despite me being in this industry for more than thirty years, every bit of their savings was in bank accounts. That's how they were comfortable investing. Financially, they were at peace with themselves right up until their final days.

In simple terms: Saving is a prerequisite for smart investing.

Saving is a prerequisite for smart investing.

BECOMING A BETTER SAVER

Money basically comes in the door one of two ways. For most people, money comes in the form of earned income, a paycheck or profit from their business. Other people are fortunate enough to have investment income, such as rental income, or dividends, or interest. When that money comes in the door, you have really only one of two choices: (1) spend the money, or (2) add it back to the pile of money you've already accumulated. Obviously, if you add it back to your savings, the pile gets bigger and therefore generates more money you can spend later (i.e., adds to your degree of freedom later in life).

As a financial planner, I can't force or guilt you into saving money. But I can introduce you to some strategies that will make it easier for you to do so.

- If your employer, for example, offers a 401(k) or similar payroll reduction savings plan, you can enroll in that plan.

- If your employer doesn't offer such a plan, most financial planners have the ability to set up a program that will automatically withdraw money each month from your checking account for investment purposes.

- Calculate what percent of your household income is saved each year. This is your benchmark. Commit to increasing that percent each year at a minimum of 1 percent. Do not think in terms of saving more dollars; focus instead on increasing the *percentage* of earnings that you save. I can't stress this enough. It doesn't matter what the number is. There's no judgment here. Just identify what percent you are now saving. Then your goal the next year is to increase that by 1 percent. If you were saving 6 percent last year, the next year make it 7 percent. The year after that, make it 8 percent. Just make sure it's 8 percent of whatever your gross earnings are in that year.

I can't force anyone to make those changes; I don't ever intend to. But I do have a role in the process. My role is to act as a mirror, to reflect back on what you are doing and to ask you to consider, "Is this what you really want to be doing, or do you want something different?"

If you don't like what those answers are, then it's my job to offer suggestions, options, and alternatives to help you change your trajectory. In doing so, we return to your financial GPS. The big questions are, "How do we get from your current reality to your vision for the future? How are we going to get there? What are the resources we've got available to utilize? What is the timeframe we have to work with?"

This is the point when it's time for my clients to do some serious self-reflection. Everyone must be brutally honest with themselves and ask questions. What is your willingness to save? Or let me put that another way. What is your willingness to moderate, control, or at least be aware of your spending? I'm not going to tell you how to spend your money. I'm not going to tell you that you can't spend it. The point here is to know yourself. Which goals are really priorities? What are you willing to do differently to achieve your priorities? What goals do you wish to modify?

In terms of your investments, what is your willingness to take risk? Knowing your willingness to deal with the uncertainties of the investment world helps us determine how best to connect these two dots. Can you get there from here, based on what you know about yourself and what you're willing to share with me? That's why the concept of a financial GPS only works when given accurate data about your current location and your desired destination. Without accurate data, your financial plan is just a guess. You really don't know what your reality is until the numbers have been run. Everything else is just a fantasy.

CONNECTING THE DOTS

Now, let's return to your financial GPS for a moment. We now know where you are today (the first blue dot on the map), and we know where the second blue dot is on the map (your destination, i.e., dreams and goals). We also know some of the lay of the terrain along the way: your financial priorities, needs, wants, or wishes.

So now it's time to use some of our financial-planning software and enter in all of those figures. This process ends with what I call a "What If Worksheet." It's an opportunity to say, "If all these things happen, will there be enough money to accomplish these financial goals?" If that gives us an unsatisfactory result, we can say, "What if you spent less? What if you worked longer? What if you got a higher rate of return?" My staff and I can create all of those scenarios.

It's just like when your GPS says, "Recalculating, recalculating." Yes, we can still get from point A to point B, but the key is finding the best route to that destination. Fortunately, there are plenty of options at our disposal:

- Save more money each year until you get to retirement.

- Work longer so you have more years to save.

- Get more aggressive with your investments.

- Spend less after you retire.

Or, to be brutally frank, you can do nothing, ignore all of this data, and run the risk of going broke and having to move in with your kids when you run out of money.

What I tell people all the time is this: "Don't get depressed if your situation isn't as grand as you'd like it to be. I'm an optimist. I know this will work out. It's just that you're going to have to change some things. Life is full of trade-offs and compromises. That's what financial planning is all about. I do know that if you've got a clear goal in mind and you know where you want to go, you have a higher probability of it working out than you would if you were unclear of the goal and how you were going to get there."

Remember, in my own life, I thought I was going to retire at fifty-five with a house on the beach. When I hatched that plan in my thirties, our reality was not anywhere close to that. Therefore, the goal was changed to the point where it became attainable.

If my wife and I wanted to retire today, we could. We probably couldn't afford to live in the house we're living in today. We might have to downsize and change a few things. But if we *wanted* to quit today, we could—and it wasn't because we ate beans and weenies for the last thirty years and scrimped and saved every dime and dollar. It's simply because we were aware of our situation and the fact that we needed to save more, and thus we become more conscious of what we spent. We did just that, and things are a lot better today.

Financial success means so many different things. What is your meaning? Because when you get right down to it, deep down, you have to ask yourself:

What are the things that are *most* important to you? If you were forced to look at your life and only give up one of these things, what would you choose?

- Your health?

- Your family?

- Your knowledge and your attitude?

- Your wealth?

If you were forced to decide between those four items, which one would you walk away from? It's all about facing your own reality and your own situation. Find out where you stand financially. Find out what's good and bad about it. Know your situation. Then make decisions.

Let me close this chapter with an important and instructive story that is dear to my heart. It's about a client named Joyce. She is a widow. Joyce and her husband had both been government employees. They had some savings and they each had a government pension. When they retired, they both took the largest pension without a survivor benefit. When Joyce's husband died, his pension died with him. She was very concerned. Was she going to have enough money?

Joyce came to us to prepare a financial plan for her. We identified the first blue dot. She told us where she wanted the second blue dot to be. When she came to our office to walk through her financial plan, she brought two daughters, a grandson, and her son-in-law. We all sat in the conference room to go through that financial plan. When we got to the "What If Worksheet," it was evident Joyce had enough money to maintain her current residence and her current lifestyle. She was going to be okay financially.

When we finished, Joyce just sat there looking at the screen. I let her sit for a second or two. Finally, I said, "Well, Joyce, do you have any questions?" She sat there for another minute or so. Eventually her daughter tapped her on the shoulder and said, "See, Mom! We told you that you were going to have enough money."

Joyce had been feeling poor. She felt like she'd lost her husband and his pension and therefore she was going to be in dire financial straits. The narrative running through her head was, "I'm broke. I need to be extremely careful. I can't spend any extra money. I can't do anything. I have to be very careful with my money." That was her narrative. Her reality, however, was very different. She didn't have money to burn. But she was going to be in fine shape, financially speaking, and it appeared she could afford to do everything she and her husband had always planned on doing. Joyce didn't believe it when her kids told her that she would be ok financially. The numbers didn't lie. Her reality was better than her narrative.

"The future belongs to those who believe
in the beauty of their dreams."
—Eleanor Roosevelt

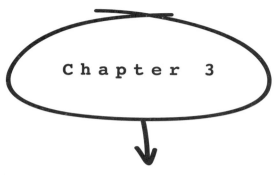

Guidelines to Understanding Money: Risk, Volatility and Portfolio Building

"Risk is not knowing what you are doing."

—Warren Buffett

As your financial advisor, it's helpful for me to know where you are coming from. During our initial meetings, I have a responsibility to gauge just how much you *really know* about money. What do you *think you know* about money or, better yet, what do you *believe is absolutely true* about money?

Unless I understand where my clients are coming from and see things from their perspective, we will be unable to construct the best investment portfolio possible. Previous experiences tend to drive current actions.

I need to know what kind of issues create financial stress as well as how you react to market fluctuations when things don't go your way. As a result, I tend to ask questions like the following:

- What is your previous investment experience?

- Why did you invest that way?

- Is your financial strategy something you came up with on your own or did someone else suggest it to you?

- How is it working out for you?

- How did you feel during the financial crisis of 2008?

- Did you change your investments during and/or after the crisis?

- What rate of return do you need to accomplish your financial goals?

I start with the past and move to the present. As part of this probing process, I've also found it helpful to ask my clients if they know their net worth. If they don't know, I can safely assume they're either very passive in regard to finances, less than fully engaged, or completely clueless. No judgment; it is merely helpful for me to know their level of engagement. I ask questions like, "If you stopped working today or if your spouse stopped working tomorrow, where would your income come from for the next year, five years, or ten years?"

It's critical that you know where your money is coming from in order to pay the bills. If you tell yourself, "Well, I'm just assuming I've got Social Security and I've got a pension, and I guess the rest will have to come from our investments." That will inevitably lead to all sorts of other questions.

- How much do you anticipate earning from Social Security? Any pensions?

- How much do you anticipate receiving from investments?

- How much are you going to spend?

I'm getting information that is necessary to help me guide people toward their dreams, their desires, and their individual definition of stability. It's also a way for me to determine if both spouses have an equal understanding of their finances.

EQUAL PARTNERS: THE IMPORTANCE OF SPOUSES

In almost every household, one spouse knows more about finances than the other. It's rarely a 50/50 situation. There's usually one person who has more knowledge (correct or otherwise) and more experience taking the lead. The important thing for me to understand is who is the decider. Who makes all those financial decisions? Who is the passive observer?

It's an important topic because it forces us to examine what will happen if there is a divorce or death. Unless both parties in the relationship are active participants, a surviving spouse will have to face that situation in some way, shape, or form in the future. Which is why, when my team and I prepare a financial plan, I require both spouses to be present.

It doesn't matter if one spouse is bored, uninterested, or spends the entire time texting the children and grandchildren—I want them in the room. After that first financial plan, if there's one person who I'll primarily be dealing with, that's fine. However, when we do the annual review of your financial plan, we always want both parties in the relationship to be at that yearly review. Just by being there, the disinterested spouse is going to gain some knowledge as to what we're talking about and what's going on. Then, in the event the disinterested party becomes the one making all the decisions someday, he or she at least had a role in that relationship.

At the outset, when I've got both people in the room, I can ask straightforward questions that will be valuable to all of us in the long run. Questions like:

- Do you keep your bank statements? Investment statements? 401(k) statements?

- If so, do you read them or merely file them away?

- Who pays the bills?

- When was your will or trust last updated, and do you know where it's located?

- How about your healthcare directive? Do you know where it's located?

- Can you find life insurance policies, auto insurance policies, or tax returns?"

Can both spouses answer these?

Take the book you're holding in your hand right now. Often, the person who chose to pick up this book already understands more about finances than his or her spouse. But what if your spouse doesn't know a lot about finances and he or she isn't interested in this stuff? How are you going to get him or her involved?

RISK VERSUS VOLATILITY

People, including many journalists, often use "risk" and "volatility" as if they were interchangeable terms. If you really think about it, there's a distinct difference between risk and volatility. Risk is the chance or the opportunity something will happen (i.e., the possibility of loss or injury). Volatility is a change in value—either up or down.

If you go skiing, what are the chances of you breaking a leg? If you invest your money in a particular mutual fund, what are the chances of you losing all or part of the money? These are risks.

Another way of looking at risk is to assess the possibility of an unfavorable outcome. Let's return to the analogy of skiing. What is the possibility the snow will be too slushy or that you will get stuck in a blizzard? Or, in financial terms, what are your chances of not earning 10 percent from your investments, or making 5 or 6 percent, or that your account will go down 10 percent in one year? What is the possibility of losing 5 percent when you thought you were going to make 5 percent?

When discussing risk, the most common fear is the possibility of the value going down. Compare "risk" in this context with the term "volatility." Volatility means an unpredictable and rapid change in value. All your investments are going to be volatile to a certain extent—some more so than others.

What is the possibility of putting money in an investment and seeing that value change in the future? Hint: The answer is 100 percent. The value is not going to remain unchanged. It's going up or down. One has a positive outcome; the other one has a negative outcome, depending upon the time frame that you set. Volatility can either be positive or negative. I don't think anyone would complain if they had an investment that was extremely volatile and it consistently trended up. The volatility everybody's worried about is consistent downward volatility.

It's all about degrees. Remember, volatility is not always a bad thing. If you're selling, downward volatility is horrible. If you have to sell when it's going down, you're going to take a loss. But downward volatility is a tremendous thing if you're buying. It's like going to the mall the day after Christmas. Everything is on sale.

What is your concern? Risk? Volatility? Risk, in my mind, is a loss that can be slower to make back. A risk is something that may be gone forever if you don't have time for your investment to recover the losses. Volatility is a change in value that may or may not be a bad thing, depending upon whether you are buying or selling.

MEASURING YOUR TOLERANCE FOR RISK/VOLATILITY

Measuring "risk tolerance" can be tricky. A scientific questionnaire gives the planner an idea as to a client's previous experience with investments and how he or she responds to financial difficulty.

In the old days, I would have a husband and wife go through ten questions. As I asked each question on the form, inevitably they'd sort of look at each other and then one person would give an answer. I'd ask the next question, and they'd look at each other again, and then one person—the same person—would give all the answers.

I soon realized I was only getting one person's opinion because only one person was talking—at least until they got into the car and drove home. To make matters worse, the questions on those old questionnaires tended to be pretty leading. I found that people, more often than not, were giving me the answers they thought they should be giving. If I asked, "Well, what would you do if the stock market went down 20 percent? Sell everything, sell your losers, do nothing, or buy?" They'd just give me a textbook answer.

This is why I prefer using an online questionnaire that is e-mailed to each partner separately. Each partner must complete his or her own questionnaire. We get responses from both parties instead of just one person. Thus, if there are different points of view, I know about it right away. It gives me a sense as to whether there are vastly different perspectives regarding risk and volatility.

The client and I each receive the report so we have the opportunity to see if certain responses fall outside the norm. It also gives us the opportunity to have further discussions and see if they misinterpreted any questions. By going through the questionnaire and the report with our clients, we can have a conversation we never had before—and thus have a much better chance of aligning the right portfolio with their risk/volatility tolerance.

PICKING PORTFOLIOS: WHICH IS RIGHT FOR YOU?

Now that we know a client's willingness to take risks and their probable reaction to volatility, we can sit down and say, "Here are sample portfolios that seem to fit your risk tolerance." When examining these portfolios, we look at the historical rates of return as well as the volatility this type of portfolio has experienced over the last fifty years.

Let's say we start with portfolio A and find that over the last fifty years, there have been two occurrences when this portfolio went down between 10 and 20 percent; three times when it went down between 20 and 30 percent; one time when it went down between 40 to 45 percent; and, finally, one time when it went down 50 percent. Now is the time for me to ask my clients, "What would you feel like if this was your portfolio?"

Would they prefer portfolio B that never went down more than 20 percent in any one year over the last fifty years? The rates of return would be very different, but the second one experienced much less severe volatility. Now the question becomes which portfolio best fits with their financial plan? Will the less-volatile portfolio produce a high enough return to accomplish their financial goals?

This is a process known as "risk profiling." We are attempting to find the optimal risk level for a client's investment portfolio. This is rather like a three-legged stool:

- **Leg 1:** Risk profiling begins with measuring the **rate of return** necessary to accomplish the client's financial objectives. This rate of return has a volatility profile. Will this volatility be within the client's "comfort zone"? The volatility of a portfolio can be identified. It is a number that can be calculated.

- **Leg 2:** How much can a client afford to watch his or her money go up and down? This is **risk capacity.** This is also a number. Example: can the client wait through a market decline before needing to sell investments to fund a need?

- **Leg 3:** The third leg on that stool is risk tolerance, or as I prefer to describe it, **volatility tolerance**. This is not a number. Can the client handle a market decline on an *emotional* level?

A conversation about risk is really a conversation about volatility—which can and will occur—and the timing of volatility is beyond our control. When discussing volatility, there are three things to remember. Let's return to the three legs of the risk stool analogy:

1. How much return do we need to take to get the job done?

2. Can you afford, financially speaking, to watch things go up and down?

3. Can you emotionally handle watching your investments go up and down?

PLAYING THE NUMBERS: CALCULATING RISK

Risk often involves an event that may or may not happen that can have a negative outcome. Some risks include:

- Am I going to die too soon?

- Could I become injured or ill or need caregivers?

- Could I become so disabled that I can't work?

- Could I become involved in a lawsuit or a car wreck?

- Will I live too long?

Don't forget the risk of running out of money. These are all risks. These events may or may not happen.

Oftentimes, events such as inflation are described as a risk. However, many people will call inflation a certainty. Things are going to cost more in the future than they do today. By the same token, some financial planners feel that increased income taxes could be a risk to future spendable income while others are certain tax rates will go up.

What are your real risks? Allow me to ask four questions:

1. What are you most afraid of?

2. What are the chances of your fear manifesting?

3. Is this fear based upon your emotional reaction to the question, or the probability of it happening?

4. Is this fear based upon the reality of your financial plan?

Some risks like those involving auto accidents, a fire in your home, disability, or death will be covered in chapter 8. For now, the question to ask yourself is whether you will have sufficient income twenty, thirty, or forty years from now. That's a real risk. It's something that needs to be quantified and measured. Again, that comes back to the financial planning process we discussed earlier. The chance of being in a car wreck is pretty small, as is the chance, for most people, that you will run out of money in the next five or ten years. However, the possibility of expenses being higher later in life is much more probable.

A thorough conversation of volatility helps us understand how you react to watching your investment value fluctuate. It helps us understand your perceived need for returns, your past experience with investments, and your understanding of risk. All of this is matched with the reality of your current financial situation and the requirements for investment returns in your financial plan.

BACK TO THE BASICS: MAKING MONEY OR NOT LOSING MONEY?

Let's return to the idea of money, investing, volatility, and risk. How does one invest to "make money," as opposed to "not lose money?"

The goal of "growth" assets is to make money. Therefore, their value will be at least somewhat volatile and have the potential to go up as well as down. "Defensive" assets are meant to have little to no volatility, and as a result will neither make much money, nor lose a lot of money.

Growth assets include:

- stocks of both US and foreign companies

- mutual funds and exchange-traded funds (ETF) that invest in stocks

- variable annuities

- real estate

In contrast, money is invested in defensive assets to avoid losing money and to retain value. Defensive assets include:

- bank accounts

- guaranteed fixed annuities

- fixed insurance products

- highly rated bonds

All these instruments generate some rate of return, but the thing we're looking for most of all with defensive assets is the maintenance of the value of the invested principal.

STOCKS VERSUS BONDS

I've come to believe that many people lack a basic knowledge of investments, especially the difference between stocks and bonds and what causes them to go up or down in value. For those of you who already understand what sets each apart, feel free to skip ahead. But for many readers, this may be the first time anybody's taken the time to explain this to you. Too many financial advisors just assume a client knows far more than he or she really does—particularly when the client just keeps nodding when the advisor is talking. When the advisor asks for questions, the client, to avoid embarrassment, has none. The client goes along with the advisor's recommendations. Finally, everyone is shocked when the client calls in a panic during the next financial crisis.

WHAT IS A STOCK?

If you own a stock, you own a piece of a company. The value of that stock goes up and down based upon both real and anticipated profits of the company. Oftentimes, the fluctuation in a stock's price is based more on the anticipation of future profits than its actual profits today. Higher profits translate to the stock value going up. Lower profits usually lead to the value of the stock going down.

If there are more people who want to buy a stock because they anticipate the company will be more profitable in the future, the price of the stock will go up. This is called speculating on an unknown future-yet-anticipated event. To put this in another context, it is like buying cheap rural desert land because you believe a major new highway is going to be built. You are hoping an exit will be built next to your property and someone will pay you lots of money to build a hotel or casino on that plot of land. This is speculating on land: buying now and hoping for a future event to occur.

Other investors are attracted to established companies that provide a good product or service. The company has a history of increased profits over an extended time frame. As the famous investor Warren Buffet often says, "We buy good companies at a fair price." Then he has the patience to allow the company to grow. This is like buying an apartment building in a good neighborhood, then waiting for property values to increase and rent to go up in order to make a profit.

Remember this, when you own a stock, you profit in two ways. One is an increase in share price. The second is a dividend. A dividend is paid when a company chooses to pay out profits to its shareholders instead of reinvesting them in the company. In many cases, dividends can be a significant portion of long-term profits. While some companies pay dividends, others do not.

Stocks trade on an exchange. You only make money or lose money on stocks when you sell them. Buying an individual stock, like Apple, IBM or General Motors, offers you the greatest potential profit, plus the largest possibility of loss because you're investing in one company. Investing in a mutual fund or ETF which invests in many different stocks will have less volatility than investing more money in a few individual stocks.

WHAT IS A BOND?

If you invest in a bond, you are making a loan to a company. You don't own a piece of the company. Just like with any other loan, whether it's your mortgage or a car loan, the company borrowing the money pays interest. If you're a lender, you receive that interest. At the end of the term of the loan, the company gives you back the money you lent to them. Your only return on a bond investment is the interest that the borrower pays. At the end of the term of the loan, the borrower returns the lender's principal.

You must understand that bonds are bought and sold on exchanges after they are issued, and prior to their maturity. These prices change. As a general rule-of-thumb, bonds fluctuate in value less than stocks in most (but not all) time frames.

Stocks are more volatile than bonds. When the economy is in a period of strong economic growth, stocks do go up in price more than bonds. That is why stocks are referred to as "**growth assets**." However, during economic "contractions" (a fancy term for recessions), bonds go down in price less than stocks. Therefore, bonds are referred to as "**defensive assets**."

MUTUAL FUNDS

A mutual fund is an investment company that will buy either a basket of stocks or a basket of bonds. A mutual fund will invest in fifty, a hundred, or even a thousand different stocks or bonds. As an alternative to investing in a single stock or a single bond (which can be quite volatile), you might buy a mutual fund, which will invest in many stocks. This increased diversification generally provides lower volatility. Mutual funds are not going to go up or down as much as individual stocks or bonds because you've got more companies or more bonds that your return is based upon.

Mutual funds are offered in two varieties. A "**managed**" fund has a person or group of people who are trying to find better stocks or bonds in which to invest. They are buying and selling to maximize returns for their investors. An "**index**" fund will buy a basket of stocks that mirror a stock index such as the S&P 500 (large companies) or Russell 2000 (small companies).

Some investors and their advisors prefer managed funds because they believe their "stock pickers" are smarter than anyone else, while others believe that over time few people can be smarter than the market—i.e. "outperform the market"—and thus prefer investing in an index fund.

While a case can be made for managed funds in some cases, research would indicate in many cases investing with an index offers equal or better returns with lower costs. Regardless, this is a personal, case-by-case decision that should only be made after a thoughtful discussion with your advisor.

EXCHANGE–TRADED FUNDS (ETF)

An exchange-traded fund, or ETF, is similar to an index fund in many ways. Usually it is a basket of stocks designed to match an index like the S&P 500. Unlike a mutual fund, which trades only one time per day at the close of market, an ETF trades on a stock exchange like a stock and can be bought or sold at any time during the trading day. Professional money managers often use ETFs as a surrogate or place-holder for a stock, and frequently trade their position. An ETF can be more volatile (in both up and down markets) than a mutual fund because it is forced to buy or sell particular stocks to perfectly match the index. However, because of the lower management fees, an ETF can be an attractive option compared to mutual funds. Talk to your advisor to find out if they are right for you.

ANNUITIES

An annuity is a contract with an insurance company. That contract offers some guarantees, which can be very attractive in regard to protecting your principal, but there are also restrictions involved. Guarantees are based on the claims-paying ability of the issuing insurance company. The main guarantee an annuity offers is that, if you decide to annuitize your contract, you will have a guaranteed income stream for either the rest of your life or a timeframe that you decide. If an insurance company is going to give you various guarantees, there's going to be some limitations on when you have access to your funds.

There are various forms of annuities that have different degrees of volatility and risk, as well as different forms of guarantees. A **variable annuity** provides stock market-like returns and volatility—plus some guarantees. There is often a trade-off of cost and benefit. Make sure you understand the contract being offered to you fully before investing.

A **fixed annuity** comes in two investment varieties. The first provides a guarantee of your invested principal and an interest rate similar to what banks are offering. The second provides the same principal guarantee, but the investment is based upon a stock index return up to a specified market cap with a guarantee of no negative return due to market fluctuations in any contract year.

The earnings inside an annuity contract are tax-deferred until taken from the contract. This is often a motivating factor for some investors. However, the income tax on these earnings will be paid by someone: either the person who purchased the annuity, or the beneficiary of the annuity.

LIFE INSURANCE

One last vehicle that is worth mentioning is life insurance. Traditionally, life insurance is not thought of as an accumulation vehicle. First and foremost, life insurance should be purchased to provide a death benefit to your survivors. However, many wealthy investors and their advisors take advantage of features that are unique to specially designed life policies. These contracts have a greatly reduced death benefit to minimize costs in order to take advantage of tax features unique to life insurance. There are no limits to the amount of money you are allowed to contribute. The money in the policy grows tax free. You're able to access the funds at any time, for any use, without limitations on a tax-free basis. Upon your death, that wealth transfers to your named beneficiary—spouse, children, anyone you choose to name—income tax free (unlike your IRA or 401(k)).

It's important to keep in mind that cash value is obtained from life insurance through policy loans and partial withdrawals. Policy loans and partial withdrawals may vary by state, generate an income tax liability, reduce available surrender value and death benefit, or even cause the policy to lapse.

REMEMBER ONE THING ...

One more piece of advice before we move on: be suspicious of any advisor who speaks in jargon you don't understand without explaining it to you. Terms like alpha, beta, standard deviation, duration, correlation, asset allocation, and sector rotation—all of these words are common parlance in the investment profession, but for a lot of laymen, an advisor who uses these terms might as well be speaking Klingon. Don't allow yourself to feel stupid or intimidated by someone who's trained, educated, and more experienced in working with money than you are.

Personally, I don't have a clue what goes on under the hood of my car or how electricity works. I do know that water gets from one end of my house to another because of pipes, but that is the extent of my plumbing knowledge. The reason I don't know a lot about any of those things is because, frankly, I don't care that much about them. That doesn't mean car mechanics, electricians, and plumbers are smarter than I am. It just means they've accrued different experience and knowledge in their fields.

Same thing with your investments. If you want to take the time to learn all this stuff, you can. If you don't want to learn all the jargon, make your advisor speak English, or better yet, find another advisor.

Despite all of our discussions about financial plans, investment vehicles, volatility, and risk, in the end, it all boils down to a few basic questions: What's important to you? Why are we doing all of this? Why are you reading this book? Why are you talking to an advisor?

Picking the right investments is really not that critical to your financial wealth. The one thing that *is* very critical is to ask yourself, "Why are you doing this? What's important to you?"

"The most important thing is the why."
—Simon Sinek

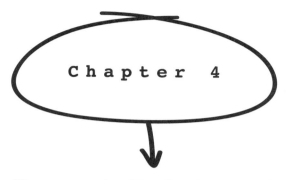

Economic Potholes and Pitfalls: How to Avoid—and Conquer—Financial Biases

"We have two classes of economic forecasters: Those who don't know—and those who don't know that they don't know."

—John Kenneth Galbraith

Allow me to open this chapter with a couple of questions:

1. Is financial planning more about finance and the economy or about psychology?

2. Why is it that the "stock market" historically returns about 8 or 9 percent and the typical investor earns about half of that?

In most cases, we think of ourselves as rational, reasonable people who make decisions based on the facts laid before us. In reality, when we're making decisions about money, our heart tends to get in the way of our brains. Emotion often trumps logic.

Far too often, people are led astray by their own personal histories. They make financial decisions based upon biases they've learned from their parents, other people, or past behavior. They wander away, step by step, from objective reality into fantasy. I see it as my responsibility to help clients reconnect with their rational selves, disconnect from their irrational biases, and stay on track regarding their financial priorities.

CONFIDENCE GAMES, RECENT LIES, AND THE TROUBLE WITH INSTINCTS

What is bias? According to *Merriam-Webster*, it's a "particular tendency, trend, inclination, feeling, or opinion, especially one that is preconceived or unreasoned." What "opinions" do you have about money? The stock market? Your financial future? Saving money? Spending money? Giving money away? Are you a good investor? Bad investor?

The first answer you give without thinking is an example of your personal "bias." This is not to judge or say it is wrong. However, ask yourself if this bias is helping or hurting you? Is the bias based upon fact or fiction?

Daniel Kahneman is the Eugene Higgins Professor Emeritus at Princeton University and Professor of Psychology at Princeton's Woodrow Wilson School of Public and International Affairs. He received the 2002 Nobel Prize in Economics for his pioneering work with Amos Tversky on decision making and how people make decisions.

I offer Mr. Kahneman's credentials to prove a point. This man is a psychologist. Yet, he won the Nobel Prize for Economics. Should you ever question whether exploring how we make decisions is important, look up what he has to say on the subject. I highly recommend his book, *Thinking Fast and Slow*.

Kahneman and Tversky concluded that our brains have two systems. **System 1** represents our bias at work. We are inclined to make fast decisions. Our focus is on the story, not the facts. As much as half of our brain operates on autopilot, and 95 percent of our behavior is based on how we "feel" or how things "appear." They coined the phrase "law of least effort" to explain how the human brain, when faced with a decision, tends to migrate toward the easiest choice.

Research compiled by Richard Thaler, professor of economics at the Booth School of Business at the University of Chicago, finds that investor behavior is based upon what he calls SIFs—Supposedly Irrelevant Factors—which are influenced by one's mood and emotions. They include variables such as the time of the day, or season of the year, and whether or not:

- you are happy or sad/depressed.

- you are hungry.

- you are well-rested or tired.

- your favorite sports team just won or lost.

- you just saw a tragedy reported on the news.

Take a moment and review how you felt when you made a bad decision in the past. Were you in a good mood? Did you just have a healthy (but not too filling) meal? Were you well-rested? Were you stressed (due to family, work, or the decision itself)? Had you been sleeping well? Had you skipped lunch?

This is part of our learning process. Take the time to review your past decisions. What has worked for you and what has not? Einstein's definition of insanity is, "Doing the same thing over and over and expecting a different result." If you don't like your previous results, consider changing your process.

Malcolm Gladwell's book *Blink* seems to extol the virtues of intuition, instinct, and gut feeling. But in a later chapter he discusses the election of President Howard Taft, who rose to the highest office in the land because he was tall, he looked presidential, and he boasted a strong-looking jaw. After his death, he was proved to be corrupt and of low moral character. History counts him as one of the worst presidents ever.

We pick our leaders based upon thirty-second sound bites. We buy cars because of their appearance and what the seats feel like. We buy a home because the neighborhood looks nice and the kitchen "is to die for." We buy a jacket because the model looked good in it in the advertisement. Investment decisions are influenced by twenty-four-hour news cycles that often consist of more opinions and entertainment than facts.

All of the action—and most major decisions—takes place in System 1. But consider, do you *really* want your financial decision made on what looks good, feels good, or sounds good, without solid data?

The brain's **System 2** is where all the heavy lifting is done. This is where data is gathered, alternatives are compared, consequences are weighed, odds are calculated, and the reception of different points of view occur. This is not where procrastination or delaying a decision happens. It is actual thinking. This is the hard work. Most people don't like to do this. Kahneman comments that most people would prefer electric shocks over being forced to sit and think about a single topic for fifteen minutes.

System 2 is the discovery of your "what" and your "why." What are your financial and life priorities, needs, wants, and wishes? What are your greatest fears? What have been some of your past experiences? This is the real heavy lifting. Why? Because you have to recognize that today's "whats" and "whys" will probably be different later. Yes, real thinking is hard work. But a successful process requires it. I encourage people to search out their own biases and their own underlying insecurities. What are you afraid of? Why?

Humans dislike uncertainty. We like the familiar, the comfortable. When I am asked what's new, I often reply: "I prefer the old, the dull, and the boring." We strive for the world to be certain, ordered, and familiar. Unfortunately, the world is not predictable—never has been and never will be.

Humans are pattern seekers. We believe in a coherent, connected world where events occur not by accident, but as the result of a mechanical cause and effect that can be tracked, documented, and explained. We are inclined to put more faith in our own genius than in luck. We don't believe in random events; our brains seek out a reason for events. We hunt for patterns to try to predict the future. But unfortunately, sometimes there are no reasons, nor are there patterns.

Allow me to provide a few examples. In the late 1990s, there was an expectation that stocks could only go in one direction—straight into the stratosphere—because that's what recent evidence showed they had done. In turn, people became overconfident in their ability to pick stocks. Everything seemed to be skyrocketing in value, so people thought they were losing out by not punching the gas pedal. That's a striking example of something called a **confidence bias**, reinforced by a **recency bias**: "I have done well up to now, so therefore I will continue to do well picking stocks." A little success can be dangerous. Be cautious of confidence bias. Highly educated individuals with success in other walks of life can be predisposed to overconfidence bias. Unfortunately, success in one field does not often translate to success in investing.

The dot-com bubble popped in a dramatic fashion in the early 2000s. The market provided ample proof that all these amateur investors didn't know as much as they thought they did. Those who fall prey to the recency bias assume that what's happened recently is going to continue to happen moving forward. An additional example of this phenomenon occurred during the financial crisis of 2008, when the stock market and real estate market fell 40 or 50 percent in some cases. People who are prone to the recency bias assumed those downturns would never correct. They hypothesize that markets are going down now and thus will continue to go down.

As human beings, our natural inclination is to run for the hills at the first sign of trouble. If you are in a crowded place and someone yells "fire," do you wait to see how big the fire becomes or do you call the fire department immediately? If you are in a convenience store and someone walks in with a gun, are you going to wait around to see what happens? If a saber-tooth tiger jumps from behind the bushes, are you going to fight the tiger? As human beings we are hardwired to run at the first sign of danger. System 1 serves humans well in times of high danger. And yes, you are going to run. In this context, System 1 keeps us healthy.

However, if your airplane develops engine problems, the boat starts to leak, or the stock market starts to decline, is your best option to parachute from the plane, abandon ship, or sell all your stocks? Experienced pilots, sea captains, and financial planners all have protocols they follow when facing difficulties. A cool head and careful consideration of options (System 2) often leads to a solution that is very different from those advocated by your initial gut (System 1) reaction.

The three biggest challenges we all face when making major decisions are:

1. **People think too fast**. Kahneman believes people are cognitively lazy. In his book he stated that 70 percent prefer electric shock to actual thinking.

2. **People think too narrowly**. They identify and articulate only half of their goals.

3. **People think too shallow**. They don't identify the why. They fail to articulate emotional trade-offs.

My goal is to help people think slower, wider, and deeper. Remember the discussion about priorities, needs, wants, and wishes from chapter 1? Go back to the list you may have made for yourself. Let's go slower, wider, and deeper:

- How will you feel when each goal is realized? What will it look like?

- What needs to happen to make each item a reality?

- What happens if, for some reason, a goal is not realized? What does this feel like? Can you accept it? Do you have regrets? Do you feel blame?

- What is the probability of each item happening or not happening?

- What are your fears? Dying too young? Living too long? Kids moving back to your house with their families? Your parents needing physical or financial care?

When it comes to finances and investments, there's always more for all of us to learn. This means getting out of System 1 and into System 2. We need to think. But there's a danger in seeking out information. Where are you looking? Who are you listening to? Beware of **confirmation bias**—i.e., only looking to information, opinions, or facts that support the opinions you already hold.

Ask yourself, *"Am I searching for new information or merely confirmation of what I already believe?"* Mark Twain wrote: "It is not what you don't know that gets you in trouble. It is what you know to be true that just ain't so that gets you in trouble." Does your viewing, reading, and listening challenge you with new ideas? Or do they merely parrot the narrative running in your head? Is this a good thing? I've always been intrigued by different points of view, different philosophies, as well as people and organizations that might disagree with what I think.

In his book, *Behavioral Financial Wealth Management*, Michael Pompian says investors are twice as likely to avoid loss than to seek gain. Like Kahneman, Pompian believes that 95 percent of our behavior is based on how we feel. Our over-estimation bias encourages an emotional response to frequent news stories. In general, we tend to focus on the story more than substance.

In other words, if you see the same thing reported on newscast after newscast, you are likely absorbing the story but ignoring the facts. If we hear that same story multiple times, we tend to believe the narrative and extrapolate the worst-case scenario. It comes at us from every direction—national news, cable talk shows, call-in radio, internet banner ads, smartphone news flashes.

Human nature interprets whatever is being said as a call to action. We seek confirmation like a moth to a flame. Our focus is on the story—not on the facts—not on the reliability of the information. People believe what they are told, especially if the person speaking has the voice of authority. Then that single person's ideas are repeated in the form of "They say ..." or "Everyone says ..."

Thinking critically and raising doubts takes hard work. Ask yourself, "Who are *they* and why are *they* right?" Remember when you were a kid? Your mother said no, and you responded with, "all the other kids are doing it, why can't I?" Then Mom passed on the wisdom of the ages: "If all the other kids jumped off a cliff, would you jump, too?" Sometimes we just need to listen to Mom.

When we see a series of cascading events, most of us start looking for pain avoidance. We have to find some relief. And of course, we start repeating the messages we've been hearing from the media, coworkers, relatives, and the voices crying out in the wilderness. In the end, we tend to misinterpret what's going to happen.

Human nature interprets whatever is being said as a call to action. We seek confirmation like a moth to a flame. Our focus is on the story—not on the facts—not on the reliability of the information.

It's just like kids with poison ivy. They are compelled to scratch their itch. Declines in the stock market tend to create the same reaction. You feel compelled to act. You might think to yourself, "It's not going to fix itself, therefore I have to fix it." But does scratching stop that itch or does it make it worse?

Your financial plan is just like the medication a doctor gives a child to treat poison ivy. Think about what the medicine does. It stops the itch long enough for the rash to heal. A good financial plan is like the salve you put on your rash. Your portfolio is a servant to the financial plan. It provides a hierarchy of values.

When markets become volatile and you become uncomfortable, you need to go back to your financial plan and realize that market volatility is factored into it. **Volatility is supposed to happen**. Take a deep breath and ask yourself, "Why am I feeling this way?" And then recognize it's normal to feel that way.

In 2008 when the stock market was down 50 percent, it was normal to feel panic. It was okay to have felt that way. But you've got to come back to the big picture. You've got to come back to your financial plan. You might be thinking, "Oh my gosh, it's down 50 percent. I have to do something." But sometimes you need to be compelled *not* to act. You need to recognize why you feel the way you do, and that the financial plan drives the portfolio; the portfolio doesn't drive the plan.

In Homer's *Odyssey*, Ulysses knew he had to sail past the Sirens. The song of the Sirens was known to captivate passing sailors who'd crash to their deaths on the rocks. Fearing that he, too, could be seduced by the Sirens, Ulysses instructs his crew to tie him to the mast and under no circumstances, no matter his pleadings, release him.

Sometimes, your financial advisor needs to have the wisdom of Ulysses. Sometimes he or she needs to help direct you away from the Sirens' song. Sometimes we need to play the part of a doctor and provide you with the medicine for your poison ivy. Yes, the rash itches and you want to scratch it. However, scratching does not help the rash heal.

Go to your planner and use the medicine he or she recommends to help you heal and not injure yourself more. Ask your planner to tie you to the mast if you need help resisting the seduction of market declines and the media feeding your emotional and mental frenzy.

My job, and our mission as financial planners, is to bring perspective in times of emotional and financial turmoil—to remember the "truths" and keep you from doing harm to your financial self.

The events in life are neutral—not bad nor good. However, it is our reactions to those events that produce either the good or bad outcomes.

Event + Reaction = Outcome

You'll find out more and see some examples of this in chapter 5.

The events in life are neutral—not bad nor good. However, it is our reactions to those events that produce either the good or bad outcomes.

We know market declines happen. We also know we cannot predict when. So the question to ask yourself is not *if* there is going to be a major market decline, but *how will you react* when the next major market decline occurs. I apologize if I sound like a broken record, but your reaction to market events will determine your financial outcome. Please read on.

"The game has its ups and downs, but you can never lose focus of your individual goals and you can't let yourself be beat because of lack of effort."

—Michael Jordan

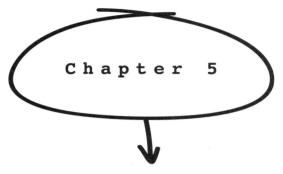

The Four Greatest Risks to Your Financial Health

"It is remarkable how much long-term advantage people like us have gotten by trying to be consistently not stupid, instead of trying to be intelligent. There must be some wisdom to the folk saying: 'It is the strong swimmers who drown.'"

—Charlie Munger

Remember the second question at the beginning of chapter 4? "Why is it that the 'stock market' historically returns about 8 or 9 percent and the typical investor earns about half of that?"

Over extended time frames, the S&P 500 (as a representation of the stock market) has averaged roughly 9 percent returns. Judging by that number, one would assume it would be easy to make money investing in stocks. You just buy today, hold it for a long time, and you're bound to make money.

Why then, according to studies published by *The Wall Street Journal* and other sources, does the average investor in the stock market only earn about 3.5 percent? Answer: Because most investors let their emotions guide their decisions.

GREATEST RISK 1: MARKET VOLATILITY

Many investors buy when everybody's excited, the companies are making money, and the markets are going up. Emotions begin with optimism, change to enthusiasm, and finally to elation. Everybody's talking about how great it is to be invested in the stock market, so they start buying, buying, and more buying as market values climb.

Unfortunately, an upward cycle always follows with a downward cycle. Growth is followed by a recession and a slowdown in the economy. Companies aren't earning more money than they did the year before, so there is a contraction. The stock market begins to decline.

As markets decline, investor emotions range from nervousness, then fear, and, finally, panic. Markets decline, the news turns negative, and people start wondering if this is going to be a recession. System 1 of the brain is saying things like, "It's different this time. It's never been like this before. I'm going to sell now before I lose any more money," or, "I am going to stop investing until it starts going up." Or, worse yet, "Well, I'm just going to get out now and wait for things to look better before I get back in."

Soon enough, investors find themselves in a vicious cycle of buying high and selling low. Rather than just waiting things out and earning 9 percent over time, they end up earning only 3.5 percent by trying to pick the "right" times to get in and out of the market.

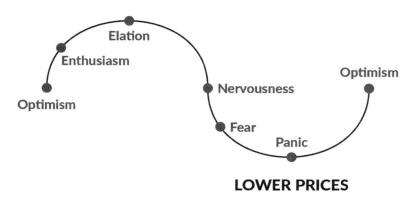

HIGHER PRICES

Elation

Enthusiasm

Optimism

Optimism

Nervousness

Fear

Panic

LOWER PRICES

Peter Lynch, the legendary manager of the Fidelity Magellan Fund from 1977 to 1990, argued against market timing, stating that, "Far more money has been lost by investors preparing for corrections or trying to anticipate corrections than has been lost in the corrections themselves."

For an example of this principle in action, consider the tech bubble of the late '90s. During that incredible stretch, you didn't have to be a smart investor to make money. All you had to do was buy large-cap stocks, particularly technology, and you were flying high. People were quitting their jobs so they could become day traders out of their spare bedrooms, and they were making a ton of money.

Suddenly the tech bubble burst, which started the recession. Then came the September 11, 2001 terrorist attacks, followed shortly thereafter by the WorldCom and Enron scandals, and markets tumbled in response to each event. This market decline lasted for almost two years.

How individual investors react to such downturns is critical to long-term success. During these boom-to-bust-to-boom periods is when investors tend to make really wise or really foolish decisions.

Let's look at some numbers to underscore this point. From 1994 to 2000, the S&P 500 was up 238 percent and 816 percent if you go back to the late '80s. How many investors were in the market for the entire time? Most jumped in during the enthusiasm of the late '90s. Then what happened? This was followed by 2001 through 2002, when the S&P 500 slid 46 percent. Why the reason for the two-year decline?

- Inflated valuation of stock values due to dot-com boom in the late '90s, followed by a recession in early 2000.

- Terrorist attacks on the US on September 11, 2001.

- Corporate lying, cheating, and stealing, leading to collapse of WorldCom & Enron.

The markets recovered, however, and over the next five years were up 108 percent. Next event: From October 2007 through March 2009 we had a housing bubble that burst, negative corporate profits, near failure of the US auto industry, and the US government intervention to prevent widespread bank failures—all adding to a very deep recession. The S&P 500 went down by 51 percent.

The conclusion? By its very nature, market volatility can either be a monetary blessing, or a danger to your financial health. But, depending on your reaction, neither result will be permanent.

GREATEST RISK 2: YOUR REACTION TO MARKET VOLATILITY, OR, THE DIFFERENCE BETWEEN A GOOD FINANCIAL DECISION AND A BAD FINANCIAL DECISION.

A decision to sell versus a decision to buy: when is one a good idea and the other a bad idea? What decisions did you and your financial advisor make during these last two recessions? Be honest. Did you have a plan in place to survive and perhaps even thrive during the periods of uncertainty? Did you ride it out waiting and hoping? Or were you running for the hills? Panicking? Buying high and selling low?

Market cycles (both up and down) always end. March 2009 provides a great example.

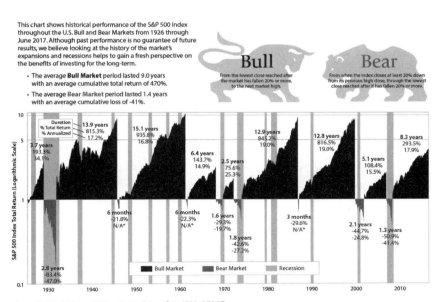

This chart shows historical performance of the S&P 500 Index throughout the U.S. Bull and Bear Markets from 1926 through June 2017. Although past performance is no guarantee of future results, we believe looking at the history of the market's expansions and recessions helps to gain a fresh perspective on the benefits of investing for the long-term.

- The average **Bull Market** period lasted 9.0 years with an average cumulative total return of 470%.
- The average Bear Market period lasted 1.4 years with an average cumulative loss of -41%.

Bull From the lowest close reached after the market has fallen 20% or more, to the next market high.

Bear From when the index closes at least 20% down from its previous high close, through the lowest close reached after it has fallen 20% or more.

Source: First Trust Advisors L.P., Morningstar. Returns from 1926 - 6/30/17.

The S&P 500 Index is an unmanaged index of 500 stocks used to measure large-cap US stock market performance. Investors cannot invest directly in an index. Index returns do not reflect any fees, expenses, or sales charges. This chart is for illustrative purposes only and not indicative of any actual investment. These returns were the result of certain market factors and events which may not be repeated in the future. Past performance is no guarantee of future results.[1]

On March 9, 2009, the stock market started to go up. Why? Because. Because why? Just *because*. The markets simply decided to go up. That's why. Did companies suddenly become profitable on that day? No. Were banks no longer in danger of failing? No. Was the auto industry selling a lot more cars? No. Were companies hiring laid-off workers that day? No. Was the recession officially over? Hell, no. So why did the stock market start to go up?

Because on that day there were more people buying stocks than selling. It had finally become obvious that the "value" of company stocks was greater than the price to buy those shares. The buying began and has continued through September 1, 2017 (as I type this) and perhaps longer. The S&P 500 is up 266 percent.

If you look within that bull market of March of 2009 to September of 2017, there was a mini bear market from April 2011 through September 2011, when the S&P 500 was down 17 percent. Most people don't even remember that, but they should.

During that time frame, Congress was unable to extend the federal debt ceiling and the federal government shut down. National parks were closed. People working for the TSA at airports had to work for free. While that was happening, Standard & Poor's lowered its rating for US government debt from AAA to AA, and everybody said, "Oh my God, here's the recession of 2008 all over again." And the markets tanked. (At least, many acted as if there was a disaster. The S&P 500 was only down 17 percent.)

---

1   "History of U.S. Bear and Bull Markets Since 1926," First Trust Portfolios L.P., Morningstar, https://www.ftportfolios.com/Common/ContentFileLoader. aspx?ContentGUID=4ecfa978-d0bb-4924-92c8-628ff9bfe12d

However, corporate profits continued to be positive; companies were making more money, and that mini recession, when the market went down 17 percent, proved to be just a small blip because from April of 2011 to September of 2017, the S&P 500 went up 73 percent.

If you look at the period from 2008 through 2009, when the markets were declining, selling your stocks would have been a bad decision. However, buying *into* a market decline can be a very good decision. So think of it this way: The real way to understand if you've made a good decision or a bad decision is to consider why you made the decision to begin with. Emotional decisions (System 1) usually lead to negative consequences. While a plan-based decision (System 2) is usually the better one.

The Great Recession of 2008–2009 showed the S&P 500 down 51 percent. What if your portfolio had some defensive assets? Would it be less volatile? By how much?

The following chart illustrates the volatility of the S&P 500 if your portfolio had some defensive assets during this recession:

100% Growth	0% Defensive	Down 51%
70% Growth	30% Defensive	Down 37%
60% Growth	40% Defensive	Down 32%
40% Growth	60% Defensive	Down 21%

Decisions, in and of themselves, are often neither good nor bad—but the reasons *why* you make those decisions often ultimately determine their value. If your decisions are based on emotion, misinformation, fear, greed, or outside influences, you may well be making a bad decision. If you make a decision based upon a well-formulated financial plan, however, then it's more likely to be a good decision. Remember System 2, not System 1.

If you talk to military personnel, first responders, and firefighters, they always have an emergency plan—a strategy for times of crisis they have rehearsed repeatedly, to the point where they can execute it without even thinking. They are not reacting emotionally. They've got a drill and they know exactly what they're going to do in each situation because they've mapped it out ahead of time.

I recommend the same type of preparation to my clients, especially when it comes to volatility. Buying into big market swings can be beneficial or disastrous, but if you follow a plan you are more likely to come out of it in better shape than if you follow your emotions.

Remember chapter 4? **E + R = O**. Event plus reaction equals outcome. Is the event positive or negative? How do you react to that event? In some cases, the best reaction is no reaction at all.

THE MOUNT EVEREST OF PERSONAL FINANCES

Consider for a moment, this mountain: Mount Everest. There have been roughly four thousand people who have successfully climbed Mount Everest. Two hundred and fifty people have died on that mountain. Do you think most of those people have died going up or coming back down?

Most people don't perish going up the mountain. They die coming back down. Why is that? My theory is that they planned, trained, prepared, and spent a great deal of energy making it to the summit. They generally don't give an equal amount of thought or preparation as to how they were going to get off the mountain.

I look at the realities surrounding Mount Everest as a metaphor for the relationships we have with our clients. My clients and I are, metaphorically speaking, engaged in a business partnership, where the clients are the chief executive officers. They're in charge. It's their money. They ultimately must make all of the big decisions. However, my team and I act as the personal chief financial officer. With the clients' input, we draft a financial plan based upon their particular needs, wants, wishes, and priorities.

As we discussed previously, the early parts of our planning process are all about identifying what is important and figuring out what our clients want to accomplish. Our job is to take the information provided to us and use it to help them determine exactly where they are today financially. We need to determine if their reality is aligned with their own perceptions. When we complete that financial plan, we charge a fee for our service. After seeing their plan, many people hire us to manage their assets as well.

The Mount Everest metaphor is apt because it's important for you to realize it's not just getting to the top of the mountain that counts. It's not just about accumulating enough money to retire. You also have to think about how to get off the mountain and back home. Our aim is to help our clients accomplish as many of their financial goals as possible—with the greatest degree of safety possible.

Some of my clients hire me because of the unique skill set that I bring to the table, in terms of managing their funds or mapping out their financial plans. But many people, quite frankly, are perfectly capable of doing what I'm doing for them. Yet, they elect to work with me because they would rather spend their time and energy doing things that they feel are more important or more fun.

They're more than willing to outsource these responsibilities to me. Financial planning is a partnership. We help our clients reach the summit (i.e., their financial priorities), but then we offer an added and equally important service: we help them get off the mountain and home safely, where they can enjoy their wealth or, if they desire, transfer it to their chosen beneficiaries.

GREATEST RISK 3: THE LONGEVITY CONUNDRUM

Although it sometimes sounds counterintuitive, one of the biggest risks to your financial health is longevity. I always ask my clients how long they plan on being retired. Most respond with an obvious answer: "Well, until I die." I would propose a different answer, namely that they're going to be retired either (1) until they die or (2) until they go broke.

Consider the facts. The average life expectancy for women is eighty-eight, and for men it's age eighty-five. But what's an average? Well, it's the typical life expectancy. Some die before the average and others later. Think about that for a second.

One extreme is the person who smokes three packs of unfiltered cigarettes every day, washed down with a bottle of whiskey. The other extreme is a person who still weighs the same as in high school, meditates, exercises daily, drinks no more than one glass of red wine in a day, and has no stress in his or her life.

In any case, it's important to ask yourself how long you're really going to be retired. Because, obviously, longevity is not the real problem. The real issue is inflation. What is it going to cost you to live if you survive that long? If you need $5,000 to cover your monthly expenses to live today—assuming you live another ten years at a 3 percent inflation rate—it's going to cost you $6,720. In twenty years, that's $9,031. And in thirty years at the same 3 percent inflation rate, you'll need $12,136 to buy what $5,000 would have bought you today. And even if you don't live that long, your spouse probably will.

When planning for health insurance premiums, deductibles, and co-pays, consider using a 6 to 7 percent inflation rate. If your health care costs are $1,000 now, in ten years at 6 percent inflation you'll need $1,791 to buy what that $1,000 buys you today. In twenty years, you'll need $3,207, and in thirty years you'll need $5,743 to buy what $1,000 worth of health care will buy you today. That's a huge factor that you definitely need to consider in your plan.

I've found that one of the biggest factors most people don't like to think about—and they sure as heck don't want to talk about it—is the cost of care should they be unable to live on their own and care for themselves. It's been estimated that between 70 and 80 percent of people who are sixty-five today will require some form of either home care or residential care before they leave the planet. The cost of that care can be staggering, especially considering that the average cost of nursing care in this country is currently (2017) $83,950 a year. And that's just an average cost.

I have a personal story that illustrates this cost in action. My mom lived for six years in an assisted-living facility in South Dakota. The last year of her life she was in nursing care. From her estate, we paid $79,000 for nursing care for that one year. The cost of care in South Dakota is relatively modest when compared with the rest of the nation. If you inflate today's cost forward, in ten years that same level of care is going to be $136,746.

Thus, you have to ask yourself some important questions regarding care costs:

- Do you have a plan?

- What's the plan?

- How are you going to pay for such services?

- Will the money come from your assets?

- Do you have an insurance policy that will cover at least part of it?

- Are your children going to have to pay for it?

GREATEST RISK 4: THE TAX MAN COMETH

Most people's default mechanism to save money for retirement is their 401(k) plan. However, there's a big reason that your 401(k) plan may not always be the best vehicle for saving. You have a partner in your 401(k) plan. That partner is the IRS. The folks at the IRS want your 401(k) to get as big as possible because they own a piece of it. They're going to get anywhere from 25 to 45 percent of the value that you've got in that 401(k) plan.

Are income taxes going up in the future or are they going down? I don't have an answer to that question, but I have a guess. Our population is aging. More and more people of retirement age are living longer. We have fewer people working relative to the number receiving benefits. Thus, there appears to be a lot of pressure on government services like Social Security, Medicare, and other healthcare programs.

Also consider the fact that we've got a $20 trillion in government debt, and interest rates have been very low for years. If interest rates go up, meaning the economy is stronger, the government's going to have to borrow money at higher interest rates than they have since

2009, which means the debt service on that $20 trillion of debt is going to cost more money.

Then there's our crumbling infrastructure: bridges, roads, hospitals, libraries, airports. They're going to have to be rebuilt. The planet doesn't seem to be much safer than it's been in the past, so don't expect reduced government military spending.

So, with all that in mind, let's ask the question again: "Are taxes going to go up? Or are taxes going to go down?"

Under current law, your three biggest tax deductions are mortgage interest, the exemption you receive for having dependent children living in your house, and contributions to your qualified retirement plans. Chances are those three big deductions will eventually diminish greatly and possibly go away completely in the future as you pay off debt, the kids move out, and you aren't contributing to your 401(k). If we get tax simplification and lower rates, you can expect to lose more deductions.

As a result, this myth about being in a lower tax bracket when you retire may not necessarily work out. In fact, in most cases, it doesn't work out at all. A lot of people will find themselves in a higher tax bracket after they retire. Which is why you need to ask yourself, "Where is my retirement income going to come from? Where's the money coming from? What part of it is tax-free? What part of it is taxable? How could higher tax rates affect that retirement income?"

Remember Mount Everest. Everybody's journey is unique. Your roadmap will depend upon how much money you've already been accumulating, where that money is currently invested, and what you do with those funds between now and the time you get off the mountain. Also, don't forget, "life happens" along your journey, and you may need a "route recalculation" more than once.

If you're still planning the trip to retirement and haven't even started to climb yet, you have a lot of flexibility. If you're at base camp and getting ready to go up the mountain, you've got a little less flexibility, but you still have plenty of opportunities to make up lost time. If you've already reached the summit, and are looking at how to safely get down the mountain, then you need to immediately begin mapping out the trip down. You need a plan and guidance on how to maneuver around volatility, bad decisions, longevity, and taxes. You should ask yourself, "What will be your mix of after-tax verses pre-tax assets at retirement? How will this affect my cash flow? What are the income tax consequences to my heirs?"

I consider my team and I to be financial guides who are uniquely equipped to help you get up and down your personal mountain. It is my job to give you options, and to help you determine where your greatest risks lie, as well as lay out potential solutions. Wherever you are on the mountain, you've got to start sometime. There is no better time than the present.

"The farther backward you can look,
the farther forward you can see."

—Winston Churchill

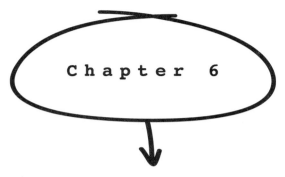

A Fork in the Road: A Guide for Pre-Retirement Investors

> "The only function of economic forecasting
> is to make astrology look respectable."
>
> —John Kenneth Galbraith

This chapter was written to directly address the needs of people who have not yet transitioned into retirement. If you're about to retire or are already retired, flip to the next chapter. For those who are still working for a living and facing the prospect of retirement five years or more in the future, this chapter is for you.

With luck, the kids are out of college and not living in your house. Your parents are still alive and in good health. You are making more money than you've ever made before. Opportunities still abound. In short, you're at another crossroads in life, and you've got some important decisions to start making.

Let's assume you have a financial plan. You've articulated your needs, wants, wishes, and priorities, but now you need to start figuring out how and where to accumulate money. What's the first place to start? Try thinking about the following three buckets. Where should you accumulate your wealth?

THREE WAYS TO BUILD WEALTH

* For qualified expenses.

The bucket on the left is for **taxable money**. The middle bucket is for **tax-deferred money**. The one on the end is reserved for **tax-free money**.

The **taxable bucket** includes things like savings accounts, money markets, CDs, and after-tax investment accounts with stocks, bonds, and mutual funds. The biggest advantage that taxable accounts offer is that all assets within them are liquid. They are available to you at any point in time. This is your "opportunity" money, or emergency fund cash, because it's available to you without restrictions or taxation. The biggest disadvantage to holding these assets is that they are taxed each and every year on everything they earn: interest, dividends, and capital gains.

Every spring, I get a phone call from clients complaining about their tax liability because of all of the interest, dividends, and capital gains they earned that year. The good thing is that they made money. The bad thing is they have to pay taxes on it every year.

The middle bucket is for **tax-deferred** money. We're talking about your IRAs, 401(k)s, 403(b)s, 457s, and TSPs. These are all pre-tax investment accounts generally offered by an employer. If you are self-employed and running your own business, you could then have a SEP, Simple IRA, or maybe a Solo 401(k). There are two big advantages to tax-deferred assets:

1. Everybody gets a tax deduction today for money they contribute to this program. The money contributed is excluded from your tax return.

2. The growth of the assets inside these accounts is tax deferred. You pay no income tax in the year that you earn money on these accounts. This allows the money to compound without taxation. This is a very, very powerful accumulation tool as there's no tax reduction on the front end, and you get all that tax-deferred growth.

However, you're not eliminating the taxes; you're merely post-poning them. It's sort of like "kicking the can down the road." Either you're going to pay the tax when you take the money out to spend during your lifetime, or whoever inherits this account—including your spouse or your children—will pay taxes on the money as was discussed in chapter 5. The only instance in which taxes aren't paid on tax-deferred assets is if you name a charity as a beneficiary and the charity receives the money from the retirement account when you die. More on this in chapter 9.

The third bucket is for **tax-free assets**, which usually includes things like Roth IRAs, Roth 401(k)s, and municipal bonds. The interest you earn on municipal bonds is, by and large, going to be tax free, at least at the federal level, and, perhaps, at the state level.

However, one thing many people do not realize is that muni-bond income is considered provisional income, so you need to check with your tax advisor to determine whether or not a large amount of municipal bond interest income will increase the amount of taxes you end up paying in regard to Social Security.

Roth-IRA, Roth-401(k)s, and Roth-403(b)s are great tools for saving money. You are contributing after-tax dollars—so there's no tax deduction on the contribution. However, none of your earnings are ever taxed because all distributions from all Roth-like accounts are tax-free to you or your beneficiaries as well as not having any required distributions. The IRS cannot require you to take money out during your lifetime. Traditional Roth IRAs have relatively low contribution limits as well as income limits. Check with your tax advisor for current limits.

Many employer-sponsored 401(k) plans may have a Roth option. You can allocate all or a portion of your $18,000 to $24,000 maximum contribution to a Roth. You pay taxes on those wages if the contribution goes in as a Roth, but everything it earns and everything that comes out later in life is going to be tax-free.

The overfunded life insurance policy discussed in chapter 3 can be an extremely powerful and useful planning tool for accumulating tax-free money. This is a specially structured life-insurance policy with a greatly reduced death benefit to minimize costs in order to take advantage of tax features unique to life insurance. There are no limits to the amount of money you are allowed to contribute. The money in the policy grows tax-deferred. You're able to access the funds at any time, for any use, without limitations on a tax-free basis. Some policies offer no-risk investing of your contribution. Upon your death, that wealth transfers to your named beneficiary—spouse, children, anyone you choose to name—income tax free.

When thinking about and comparing tax-deferred vs. tax-free investments, it may be helpful to consider the analogy of a farmer or a factory owner. If you were a farmer or a factory owner, would you rather pay income tax on the seeds you plant—your raw materials in the factory—or would you rather pay income tax on your crop, or products, when they are sold?

That's the difference between a tax-deferred account and a tax-free account. Do you want to pay taxes on your raw materials or do you want to pay taxes on the end product? Again, the answer depends on your particular situation.

With any investment or saving program, be certain you fully understand all fees, costs, and "gate-keepers." Is your advisor held to a "suitability standard" where they only have to ensure their recommendations are suitable or are they held to a "fiduciary standard" where they are required to act in your best interest? Does your advisor own the same investments they are suggesting to you? Or, at the very least, does their mother have the same investments?

FINDING THE RIGHT BALANCE

My aim when working with clients is to provide a path for them that provides optimum flexibility given the utilization and spending of money they've already accumulated. Often the best approach is to encourage them to put half of their money into pre-tax accounts, like 401(k)s, IRAs, etc., where they get a tax break going in and then pay taxes after retirement. The other half of their money should be in after-tax or tax-free accounts, like after-tax investment accounts, savings, Roth IRAs, or an overfunded life insurance policy.

This mix provides flexibility. It's very common for people to focus solely on tax-deferred accumulation. But the problem comes when they're ready to retire. If every dollar they've accumulated is in a pre-tax account, they're going to have to pay taxes on every dollar that comes out of that account.

With a balance between pre-tax and after-tax assets, the tax impact during retirement can be better managed. A mix of tax-deferred, taxable, and tax-free investments allows for blended distributions when you're taking out money on a monthly basis to fund your lifestyle. What if you need $50,000 or $100,000 in a lump sum? If you need $100,000, you might need to take $140,000 out of that IRA deferred account to net $100,000, whereas if you've got money that's already in a tax-deferred account or a tax-free account, all you have to do is take out $100,000 because you don't have a tax issue to worry about.

My point, of course, is that you can't gloss over the fact that the money you spend now will have repercussions for you down the road. The options you will have in retirement are a product of the decisions you make prior to retirement.

If you're making more money now than you've made before and your expenses are down because you're not paying for your children's college educations anymore, what are you going to do with that extra money? You can start spending the bonus money you got last year, or the money you've been giving your kids for college, or that inheritance from Aunt Tilly, and enjoy it now—or you can save it, let it compound, and enjoy it over a longer stretch of time when you're retired. None of those choices are good or bad, but they do have consequences. If you make those decisions without a plan, you'll be guessing as to what the nature of those consequences will be.

THERE ARE ONLY TWO WAYS TO MAKE MONEY

In the real world, there are only two things that make money: (1) a person who is working for money, and (2) money at work making money. The question is: how much money do you need to have working for you to allow you to stop working for money?

If you want to stop working for money, if you want to get out of the rat race, you are going to have to come up with a plan to accumulate some money, so it can start working for you. Thus, the answer is not really how much of a return you can make on your money, it's more of a question of how much you decide to save. There's no judgment here. There are just decisions that you have to make.

Allow me to tell you two stories. The first one involves a man who had spent twenty years in the military. When he retired, at a pretty young age, he began receiving a military pension, and he then went to work for the federal government. After being poor for all those years in the military, he and his wife decided to not only spend the money he was earning as a federal employee but also his pension. Life was good.

He worked for the federal government until he earned a second pension, and then he went to work in the private sector. Now he drew a salary from his private-sector job, his military pension, and his federal pension. Life was even better, as he and his wife managed to find a way to spend all of that money. Over the years, this couple bought bigger houses and nicer cars for themselves. They had a spectacular country club wedding for their daughter. They helped the kids buy houses. They travelled the world. They lived a great life.

I first met this client when he had finally decided to stop working and become permanently retired. At that point, he and his wife were left with his military pension plus his federal pension and a few hundred thousand dollars they were able to accumulate in various tax-deferred retirement accounts. But in effect, they were looking at about a 50 percent reduction of income.

It wasn't a bad life. The pensions provided a good retirement income. But they had to face the fact that the cost of living on those pensions in the future was probably not going to allow for the same standard of living that they had enjoyed previously. They would need to be careful with their spending and probably downsize from that last big house they bought, and no more luxury cars because the amount of savings was not enough to replace the wages from his last job. No more exotic travel. No more big gifts or educations or weddings.

This change of lifestyle was not really a surprise. They sort of knew a reduction was coming; they just didn't realize how much. Some advanced planning would have given them options and alternatives to consider. Maybe they wouldn't have changed a thing. Maybe they would have chosen to live the high life all those years without regret. But, then again, maybe not. In this case I was not given the opportunity to provide them with pre-retirement planning or, to borrow some medical parlance, offer any kind of preventative care. I was like a cardiologist who was being called in after the heart attack to fix the damage and save the patient. I came bearing bad news: they had to cut their spending by 50 percent.

The second story involves a couple who, when they were first married and starting to have a family, lived on just one salary. The mom took care of the children until the youngest entered preschool. When she went to work part-time at a daycare facility, the family decided to continue to live on one salary—the father's—as best they could. They did increase some of their expenses, such as moving from a condo to a nice family-friendly home, but by and large they lived on that one salary.

A few years later, Mom got a teaching job. They had a good time that first year and enjoyed their extra income. But then they opened a retirement account and started to contribute 15 percent of her salary to it. They increased that percentage every year until they got to the maximum allowable contribution.

They moved to the country, so their expenses went up a bit, but they still continued to save money. They switched some of their pre-tax savings into a Roth option because they knew they wanted more money to be tax-free after they retired.

When the kids went off to college, they paid for those expenses out of excess cash flow, all while continuing to save. Every time they would refinance any of their real estate to get a lower rate, they would take the reduced payment and use that money to overfund a life insurance policy, a concept we talked about earlier. The idea was to accumulate as much money tax-free as they could.

When the bills for college stopped coming and they found themselves with an extra $25,000 or $30,000, they started a second life insurance policy and overfunded that instead of spending their newfound wealth. So, by and large, their lifestyle only consumed a portion of their increased income. They were, therefore, able to sit back and let a meaningful amount of their money work for them.

My point is this: If you have time before you retire, sit down with your plan and your financial advisor and begin to make choices. The choices you make are entirely up to you. You can live a great life now and have all the fun that your income is able to generate. There's nothing intrinsically wrong with that. Or you can save more money now to have greater security later.

You need to ask yourself, do you want to make all your money by working and depend on Social Security and maybe a pension when you retire? Or do you want to have investment assets that can add a meaningful amount to your other retirement income? Ultimately the choice is up to you.

"Money is a terrible master
but an excellent servant."

—P.T. Barnum

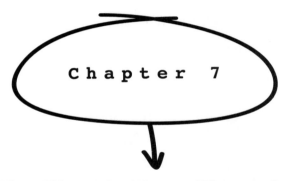

Chapter 7

The Time Is Now: Financial Strategies for the Retirement Years

"Someone is sitting in the shade
today because someone planted
a tree a long time ago."

—Warren Buffett

This chapter is written specifically for people who are close to retirement or who have already retired. If you find yourself in either of these stages in life, it's vital to begin taking a good hard look at how you're going to manage your cash flow for current expenses and for future unanticipated events.

It's a necessity that all retirees and near-retirees map out their income and spending plans at least three years in advance of the date they stop working. Remember, three years is the magic number.

I'll explain why you should plan that far in advance—but in order to begin you should return to your financial GPS. As mentioned earlier, it's important to periodically see where you are on the map and where you want to be moving forward. You need to assess what your current spending levels are so you can determine how best to invest for the future.

Begin by identifying what your revenue sources will be in retirement. Where are you going to get the money you'll need to live on? For most people, retirement revenues are drawn from four different places: pensions, individual retirement accounts (IRAs), organic/investment income and, of course, Social Security.

Different investors will have invested in different vehicles over their lifetime, but often it's how—and when—you begin to draw from these various buckets that can have the greatest impact on your retirement. Let's break down each of these revenue sources and discuss some suggestions about withdrawals from each.

PENSIONS

Though increasingly rare today, pensions provide retired workers with fixed monetary payments during retirement. People who have pensions today are usually government employees (city, federal, and state workers) as well as teachers, police officers and fire fighters. A few individuals who began working in the private sector many years ago may also have a small pension. If you do have a pension, it's important to make a *very* careful decision regarding survivorship benefits before you retire. A pension benefit for your life only will be bigger than a benefit that continues after your death to your surviving spouse.

RETIREMENT PLAN DISTRIBUTIONS

As discussed in previous chapters, retirement income includes money that can be withdrawn from both Roth (tax-free) accounts and traditional pre-tax IRA/401(k) accounts. One of the key issues to explore here is timing. Most people say they want to defer all the taxes on their pre-tax money for as long as possible. But sometimes that's simply poor planning.

For pre-tax accounts, the IRS requires holders to begin taking distributions at age seventy and a half. The minimum distribution each year is based on your life expectancy. So, at some point, the taxman is going to force you to take money out, and he's going to tell you how much of it you have to take out.

When you are age seventy and a half, the IRS assumes you have a twenty-seven-year joint-life expectancy with your spouse. So, the first year, you take the dollar amount that's in the account at the beginning of the year and divide by twenty-seven. The next year divide by twenty-six, and then by twenty-five and twenty-four and twenty-three and so on down the line.

What the IRS is doing is forcing you to take money out of your account over what is, in actuarial theory, your life expectancy. But here's a key point to consider: If all your assets are in a pre-tax account and that account has a large value, you could be forced to take out more money than you need (or want) to take out. You have no options to *not* take the money out. You will have to take out the minimum and you will have to pay taxes on it. Therefore, in some cases, it makes sense to start taking money out *before* you get to seventy and a half.

FYI: if for some reason you "forget" to take out the minimum required, the penalty is 50 percent of what you should have taken out plus taxes on the entire amount you should have taken out. Ouch!

Timing is everything. Remember, every cent of your pre-tax money will be taxed when it comes out, regardless of whether you, your spouse, children, or beneficiaries take out the money. Smart income-tax planning can be extraordinarily important in making sure you or your loved ones keep as much of your hard-earned money as possible. As an example, if Mom is in a lower tax bracket than the kids, it may make sense for her to take larger IRA distributions during her lifetime even if she doesn't "need" the money and pay taxes at her lower tax bracket rather than trying to leave as much in the account as possible which could result in her son, the surgeon, paying taxes at his highest tax bracket.

ORGANIC INVESTMENT INCOME

This includes interest, dividends, and rental incomes (if you own real estate) that your portfolio generates all by itself. This income is usually predictable and does not vary dramatically from year to year. Yes, rentals can have a vacancy, interest rates change, and dividends can be reduced—but overall this "organic" income is predictable.

SOCIAL SECURITY

Most people receive Social Security payments, but few know how to maximize returns from the system. Today, full retirement age for people is either sixty-six or sixty-seven, depending on the year they were born. For further details, go to www.SSA.gov.

For most people nearing retirement, the question everyone wants answered is "When should I start taking my Social Security payments?" There are options abound and it seems everyone you ask has an opinion. You can take Social Security at full retirement age. You can receive a reduced benefit as early as age sixty-two. You can also delay taking it until age seventy. Your decision should be based on your own financial situation. But there is some important information about Social Security that everyone should consider.

If you start taking your Social Security before your full retirement age, that benefit will be reduced by 8 percent each year before the advent of your full retirement age. In other words, if you elect to take Social Security at sixty-two, rather than at your full retirement age of sixty-six, you're looking at a 32 percent reduction of your Social Security benefit. This can have a huge long-term impact on your finances because all subsequent cost-of-living increases are based on the amount you receive when you *start* taking Social Security.

If you delay taking Social Security beyond the full retirement age (up to age seventy), that benefit increases by 8 percent each year—for every year that you delay. When I mention delaying Social Security I am often asked, "What happens if I die young?"

The answer? Yes, if you delay benefits and die before age eighty, you will have left some money on the table. That is bad luck. However, the advantage of receiving larger benefits if you don't die young over the long term can be immense. How much are we talking about? Ask an expert to run your numbers—calculate total benefits received beginning at age-sixty-two, beginning at age sixty-six, and beginning at age seventy, assuming you live to age eighty, age eighty-five, and age ninety respectively. Don't forget to add in cost of living increases to each scenario.

It's also important to consider spousal benefits, especially if one spouse has a significantly higher Social Security benefit than the other. The rule is as follows: When the first spouse passes, the surviving spouse will receive the larger of the two benefits. It's important to remember that your (or your spouse's) benefit can continue for thirty years or more after retirement.

EARLY PLANNING: THE THREE-YEAR RULE

As mentioned, I want to stress the point that it's important for retirees to begin looking at cash flow, investments, and Social Security payments at least three years in advance of retiring. Why so far in advance? Because, as a rule, you will not want to be placed in a situation where you are forced to sell investments to meet cash-flow or emergency needs. Financial wealth is preserved by planning money needs in advance. Life is unpredictable; that is why I make every effort to plan for contingencies.

Whatever your current financial situation—whether you're doing well, have average savings, or see trouble on the horizon—you need to make sure you never paint yourself into a corner where you have to sell an investment when you don't want to. If you fail to analyze your cash flow or to ensure you have enough reserves for emergencies, you won't have the ability to sell when you want to sell—i.e., when it's the most prudent time for you to do so.

Warren Buffet has become rich and famous. He buys when others feel the "need" to sell. Avoid selling because you "need" to. Sell when it is good for you and within the guidance of your financial plan. Remember the "Three-Year Rule."

For example, you have a portfolio that's 70 percent invested for growth. In such a case, market downturns usually range from two months to as long as two years. But that's just the downswing. You'll need to wait for it to go back up as well. Recovery periods for growth portfolios also usually take anywhere from two months to as long as two years. In most cases, from the top of the market to the bottom and back to the recovery point is usually a three-year period. Plan your income and cash-flow strategy three years in advance, and you'll have the ability to ride out a downturn right back to where you started.

The great thing about the three-year rule is that it covers other allocation models as well. Say you have a portfolio that's invested 40 percent for growth. In such a case, market downturns tend to last only a year or less with a recovery period spanning about a year or less as well. So the full cycle, historically, could last long as three years, but more likely two years. If you've planned three years in advance, however, you'll be covered. You should not have to sell any assets as the markets try to recover.

Unfortunately, many retirees don't take into account that they are bound to experience a number of these market fluctuations during their retirement years. I call it the "green banana" effect. Some people in their seventies have said to me, "Honey, I am old. I don't buy green bananas anymore." But as we've discussed, if you're seventy years old, you've still got a 50 percent chance of making it to ninety. Chances are, you will have a potential for bushels and bushels of green bananas in your future.

This topic is so important that it's worth repeating: If you have to sell when the market is down, you've put yourself in a very bad position. To avoid the negative affect of market volatility, you *need* to plan ahead. However, if you're going to live another twenty years, you *cannot* invest your money in a way that only protects your principle. You cannot invest 100 percent of your money in "safe" guaranteed investments. Unless you have lots of money, you will probably have to get a return greater than inflation to protect the purchasing power of your assets as well as your legacy.

This is why it's so important to divide your resources four ways for use in different time frames:

1. the money you will be using for the next three years—no risk, no volatility.

2. the money you will need in a three- to five-year timeframe—low risk, low volatility, some return.

3. the money you need in a five- to ten-year timeframe—moderate risk, moderate volatility, better return.

4. the money you won't need for at least ten years or longer—more volatility, returns greater than inflation plus taxation.

Once you've made those divisions, you can treat each bucket of money differently. The money you're not going to need for a while can be invested in vehicles with higher volatility and potentially greater returns. Why would you take this risk? Because there's a good possibility you're going to need greater returns to pay for the larger expenses (think healthcare) that will hit twenty years from now.

It all goes back to your financial GPS. As you travel along your journey, you will need to recalibrate. The longer you live, the better chance you'll keep living even longer. So you keep recalibrating. You need to try to anticipate your journey moving forward. If you look at statistics in terms of average survival rates, you should assume you've got a long journey ahead.

Allow me to give an example. You are in the car driving to a destination you have not visited before and are bit unsure how far away it is or how long it takes to get there, due to traffic or road construction. Your gas tank is just under half full and you are passing the last station prior to your destination. Do you stop and fill up, or do you drive by, thinking, "If I run out of gas before my destination I will walk the rest of the way"?

You are seventy years old. Does your financial plan cover you to age eighty? Eighty-five? Ninety-five? What happens if all your investments are "guaranteed" and your money lasts to age eighty but no longer? How much longer will the money last if the investment mix changes? Life is full of compromises and trade-offs. Consider *all* your options.

Once again, you have a responsibility to remind yourself: What is your desired destination in retirement? What are your needs, wants, wishes, and priorities *right now*? Then keep recalibrating and rewriting your financial narrative and your financial plan.

If you're now retired or on the verge of it, you will want to redefine your priorities, needs, wants, and wishes. You may need to ask yourself: "What are you willing to sacrifice if it turns out you *cannot* have it all?" That's a very, very important answer. Remember, you're going to have one set of needs now and a different set later. Take another look at the section on needs, wants, and wishes way back in chapter one. Try to articulate what these are in your life. It is important to articulate these as clearly as possible.

THE INFLATION EFFECT

Let's look at some statistics to observe the effects of inflation over time. Normally the inflation rate is 3 percent on most expenses. With health care, however, I tend to use an inflation rate of 6 to 7 percent. According to some statisticians, though, even that rate may not be high enough. As I write this (2017), the future of health care costs is very much uncertain.

Once again, life expectancy calculations are a key factor. How long will you live? I have discussed this before, but it bears repeating. To gain a better understanding of this, I recommend you go to www. livingto100.com/calculator. The site will ask you twenty-five or thirty questions and then, based on your answers, give you a better idea of what your life expectancy might be. Don't overlook the big unknowns, like long-term care. Seventy percent of people are going to have to pay for some kind of care before they leave this world.

Financial plans allow you to see where you really are in terms of income and savings, not where you think or hope you are. Once you come face to face with reality, you can start making sound decisions. If the plan is not looking great, one option, obviously, is that you can begin spending less right now. You can downsize to a smaller home. You can stop going on vacations or curtail some of your traveling. Maybe dump the big motor home or the luxury automobiles that you've been using up till now.

Another option would be to maintain your current lifestyle and spending habits, knowing that at some point in the future you're going to have to dramatically change your ways. This is not a bad choice, as long as you're doing it knowingly.

Some people may choose to begin making lifestyle changes immediately, while others might opt to maintain the current lifestyle and wait to make more dramatic moves later. The third option is probably one that few people are excited about, and that's moving in with their kids. You supported them for eighteen to twenty-five or maybe even thirty years. Maybe it is their turn? (Joking! Or am I?)

Let me recount an instructive story here. I was talking to a client of mine, around the time my oldest child started college. We were talking about the much higher expense of a college education relative to when we went to college "back in the day." My client, Bill, was a very successful business consultant. This was the second marriage for both him and his wife. Between the two of them, they had six kids. They had elected to pay for five years of college for each kid. That's thirty years of college, which cost them almost $1 million in total.

Bill was looking forward to retiring soon, and we were discussing financial planning as it related to his situation. After spending so much money on his children's educations, his options were to (a) work longer, (b) dramatically change his lifestyle when they retired, or (c) my suggestion: join with his wife, a year before retirement, in sending out a letter to each child with their annual Christmas card.

The letter would inform his kids that retirement was coming in a year or two and their plan for retirement was to live with each of their children one year for every year that Mom and Dad supported that child while he or she was in college. If you figure that they're going to spend thirty years in retirement and they funded thirty years of college, that should pretty much be their retirement plan.

Of course, I was only partially serious. Bill never sent the letter, but the story underscores the point that life is often a tradeoff. Retirees without sufficient resources to "do it all" can either downgrade their lifestyles now, dramatically alter them later, or, perhaps, find themselves having to move in with their children at some point in the future.

The important thing to realize is that you and your partner should contemplate and discuss these issues early on. What's important to you? Not what's nice or what you might like your life to be like, but what's *really* important. You have to ask yourself, "At the end of my life, if I've got to give up something, what am I willing to give up?"

Is maintaining your lifestyle important or is being around your family more important? Is your health more important than your money? Life is filled with decisions that should be evaluated based on the options and alternatives you have available to you.

Unfortunately, many people are forced to make decisions out of necessity. I'm not saying that a financial plan will make your life great, grand, and glorious. Nor am I saying that all of your dreams will come true. However, a financial plan could make the journey smoother, more predictable, and less stressful.

THE MONTE CARLO ANALYSIS: HOW TO APPROACH SPENDING IN RETIREMENT

When it comes to the markets, volatility, rates of return, and spending, there's no such thing as a sure thing. Oftentimes, people ask me, "How much can I spend out of my investments each year?" There are a few different ways to look at that question. Investment returns are never consistent from year to year. We have evidence that the stock market has averaged anywhere from 8 to 11 percent a year, depending upon which timeframes and which index you're looking at. But that's just an average.

The "sequence of returns"— i.e., the order in which your investment returns occur—is critical in determining whether your plan will work out for you personally. Your average return may be 8 percent, but if you make 10, 15, or 20 percent in the first four years, you're way ahead of the game and you'll have plenty of money. However, if you average 8 percent, but your first four years are negative 10 percent, negative 8 percent, zero, and negative 6 percent, this slow start has a dramatically negative impact on your overall result. This is one key to the answer as to how much you can reasonably spend out of a portfolio.

As I said before, averages are very dangerous because they're not consistent. One of the traditional, seat-of-the-pants estimates often used by advisors is to tell people they can expect to spend 3 to 4 percent of the value of their portfolio each year in retirement. Oftentimes, that rule of thumb works simply because the portfolio—based upon allocation and risk/volatility tolerance—could be making 6, 7, 8, or 10 percent returns. If you're only spending 3 or 4 percent, that means a certain amount of your return is being added back to your principal and you're dealing with a larger pile of money each year.

The reality is that if you decide you are going to spend 8 to 10 percent per year out of your portfolio each year, you are probably depleting it. The most sophisticated method of determining what's a safe spending rate for you is to have an advisor run something called a **Monte Carlo Analysis**. Engineers are often familiar with this concept.

With a Monte Carlo Analysis, a calculation is made using ten thousand different sequences of return, which is then used to calculate the "probability" that you will have enough money to last your entire lifetime based on specified spending, investment mix, and inflation rates. Simply put, the Monte Carlo analysis elevates financial planning from an "art form" to a "scientific study" of how to best cover your needs for the rest of your life.

What you don't want to do is just blindly guess as to whether you'll have enough money for retirement. If you have only one spending goal (buy a car, a boat, etc.), you either have enough money or you don't. But retirement—like life—involves a constant stream of variables. Multiple goals. Multiple wants. Multiple dreams. Inflation. Sometimes tradeoffs are required. I've had some people tell me, "I want to pay for that expensive wedding, and I'm willing to give up travel to make it work." If that's their desire, we can run our Monte Carlo Analysis to determine, yes/no/it works/doesn't work.

I'll have other people say, "Well, I'm not going to give up on my travel, so I want to downsize the wedding. What should our budget be?" Or they'll say, "We're going to remodel the house, and we want to take at least three trips during our lifetime; paying for the wedding is totally optional. How do we make that work?" Using our Monte Carlo Analysis, we're able to provide you with a probability as to whether your plan will work.

Return to your financial GPS analogy for a moment. Although you might have your sights set on a certain destination in retirement, you'll likely make a few stops along the way. Which stops interest you the most? That decision is up to you, but you must take into account there will likely be unexpected construction or road closures along the way. On a regular basis, you're going to need to recalibrate and maneuver around those pitfalls to reach your ultimate destination.

It's an ongoing process. You can map out everything you'd really like to do, everything you want to see, every place you want to stop, and then as you're doing this analysis, and working with the Monte Carlo, you find out what's reasonable and what isn't. What's a wish? What's a need? What's a want? And then ultimately, what's a priority? Then life happens. Time to recalibrate.

BACK TO THE THREE-YEAR PLAN
AND CASH-FLOW PLANNING

Example: Let's say that your normal living expenses are about $50,000 a year, and you're receiving $25,000 a year in Social Security, $7,000 a year of pension income, and investment portfolio organic income of about $8,000. All together that's a total of $40,000 a year—a shortfall of $10,000. Where's that $10,000 going to come from? The obvious answer is your investment portfolio and retirement accounts.

Remember it's critical to never sell anything out of necessity. So, in effect, if you know you're going to have a $10,000 deficit, you're going to want to set that money aside in a very low-risk position knowing that you're going to be spending that money each year. You plan that out three years in advance. Three years at $10,000 per year, or $30,000. When the stock market is up, you decide to sell some of your investments that have been profitable and set aside the money, knowing you'll be spending $10,000 per year. Each year the stock market gives you a profit, you sell to resupply your three-year needs. In years when the stock market is down, you don't sell anything—because you don't "have to"—and wait to sell when it is in your best interest.

One example of this theory in action involves Mary, who has been a client of mine since 1983. Her major asset is an IRA that was her husband's. He died sixteen years ago. She takes money from this IRA every year, in addition to her other income, to support her life.

Recently when I reviewed her portfolio, the IRA was worth $660,000. Late in 2007, before the financial crisis/recession, the account was worth $750,000. From late in 2007 through 2016, she had spent $350,000. Yet the account was still worth $660,000!

However, the big takeaway is that we had a statement in October of 2007 that showed $750,000. Fifteen months later, February 2009, the statement said $450,000. Since 2007, Mary spent $350,000. How was it possible that the account was still worth $660,000? By carefully mapping out where your money is coming from before a financial disaster hits. It's about avoiding the need to sell something in the middle of a financial disaster.

In the end, everybody's situation is unique. There are no guarantees. But what's undeniable is that your plan should drive your portfolio. Simply put, advance planning and having an action plan to follow gives you a much higher probability of success.

If you have sufficient resources to cover your needs, wants, wishes and priorities, and there's plenty of money to still pay for your bills until you're 105, congratulations! If your situation is not as positive, then you have choices to make. In either case, congratulations on discovering your reality.

"Wealth is the ability to
fully experience life."

—Henry David Thoreau

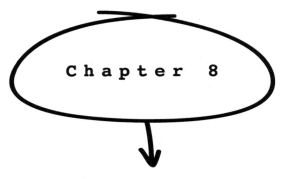

Chapter 8

What's Yours Is Yours: Protecting Your Assets

"There is nothing new in the world
except the history you don't know."

—Harry Truman

Sometimes, when you least expect it, life can absolutely blindside you. I've seen it happen countless times over my career. For years, hardworking folks did everything that was asked of them. They committed themselves to their jobs. They saved. They accumulated assets. And then, suddenly, without rhyme or reason, they found themselves embroiled in a wholly unexpected and undeserved financial catastrophe.

Some things in life—whether we like to admit to it or not—are simply beyond our control. There's no use burying your head in the sand because that won't help. Sure, you can try to mitigate your losses should these events occur. You can deflect. You can insure yourself against them, but you won't be able to prevent them from happening. Creating wealth and preserving it require two very different skill sets, which is why it's critical for everyone to carefully weigh potential difficulties that lie down the road.

Unfortunately, if you're a high-income earner (or merely work in a profession that's perceived to be a high-income line of work), you've got a target on your back. Sometimes it's a lawsuit or a divorce. Sometimes it's a car accident or a business breakup or the sudden onset of a debilitating illness. The potential pitfalls are endless, but there are several potential safeguards worth exploring.

Here are some risks I encourage my clients to consider:

- lawsuits

- divorce

- business breakup

- business failure

- loss of pension

- sudden disability

- unexpected death

Consider this chapter to be a reminder that bad things can indeed happen to you. Instead of waiting for them to happen and dealing with the fallout, be proactive and develop a plan that can help insulate you against the unforeseen in life.

OPEN YOUR UMBRELLA

When we talk about protecting one's "financial assets," we're talking about anything you would put on a financial statement. The assets that immediately come to mind for most people include retirement accounts, IRAs, 401(k)s, after-tax investments, mutual funds, money in the bank, and a stock portfolio. But one's assets can also include a home or a business plus the cash value in the life insurance, as well as pensions and Social Security benefits. It's important for everyone to look at these assets and determine how important each is to the financial survival of you, your spouse, or your children. That's where you start, determining how valuable each asset is to you now and in the future.

The best long-term strategy in terms of protecting your assets is to closely consider the probability that each of the above pitfalls might occur to you. What are the odds of something bad happening? Living in constant fear is not the answer. Fear can paralyze you and wind up doing more harm than good, but you can take a logical approach to what you want to safeguard and move along from there. Think of it as a three-step process:

1. What is the probability that a tragic event will occur?

2. What is the extent of the possible damages?

3. What is the potential cost of insulating yourself against potential losses or transferring the loss to someone else like an insurance company?

Take your home, for example. If you're concerned about the risk of your home being destroyed by fire, that's a rational concern. The chance of a fire destroying your home, statistics tell us, is around 3 percent. Although that's not exactly a large percentage, when you consider just how expensive it is to rebuild a home, finding a way to bump up your insurance coverage as your home appreciates is often a wise decision.

About 18 percent of us will be involved in an automobile accident during our lifetime. That's a pretty high percentage. Car insurance is a requirement in order to drive. But what few people fail to consider is just how much they can be sued for if they get into an accident.

Most of us will have liability insurance for our automobiles and our homes, but as a rule, the limits of liability tend to max out around $300,000 or $500,000. Those might sound like large numbers, but in reality most judgments for automobile accidents are often much higher. Often judgments start at a million dollars and go up from there.

That is why it's critical, especially if you're a high-earner, that you consider the importance of taking on a million-dollar umbrella policy that provides a million dollars in coverage above and beyond the limits of your automobile policy and your homeowners insurance. The general cost? About $300 a year per $1 million of coverage. Some of you, after consulting with your financial advisor and attorney, may want to consider a two, three, or five million-dollar umbrella policy.

Although a lot of people will say that's not exactly cheap, think for a moment about those warranties that are offered at major electronics stores. If you bought a $2,000 home entertainment system and the store offered you the extended warranty for $100, would you buy? Maybe. Maybe not. You'd have to gauge whether it was likely that your new piece of equipment would die suddenly and whether you could come up with $2,000 to replace it.

As a possible solution, consider an umbrella insurance policy. If you were involved in an accident and sued for major damages, could you cover the cost of your defense in court and dishing out over a million dollars in the settlement? Probably not.

As an example, consider a client of mine. Bridget was making a legal—and I do stress *legal*—left-hand turn at an intersection, but because she was making a left turn and the oncoming car was going straight, she was deemed to be at fault. The only reason she has assets today is because she had an umbrella liability policy that covered the judgment against her.

In many cases, it's worth insulating yourself against huge losses by taking the $300 hit for the premium every year. The potential impact of an unforeseen disaster is simply too great to ignore.

THE INSURANCE QUESTION

One of the greatest risks we are all likely to face also happens to be the one risk few people want to talk about. That's the prospect of experiencing ill health as we get older. Most people fear market dips that can disrupt the ability for their money to work for them. However, the far weightier concern should be the possibility that you or your spouse will no longer be able to work, either through death or disability.

As uncomfortable as it may be, you must consider what will happen if you become disabled or die. How vital is the revenue stream that you are generating from work? Could your partner or family members replace that revenue stream or live without those revenues and still find a way not to dramatically alter their lifestyle?

Chances are the answer to that question is a resounding no. I like to use the phrase "keeping the family in their own world." In other words, if one of the two spouses in a household is unable to work, either due to death or disability, how do the remaining family members "stay in their own world"? The importance of this applies to a great number of different types of families. It could affect a young family with small children. It could apply to people who have kids in college or someone who is already retired.

If you lose that revenue stream because the person who was working is now dead or disabled, how much money do you need to replace that revenue stream? That's a principle I call "money at work." Let's look at some numbers that bear out the potential effects of this income loss. If that loss of income is, say, $36,000 a year, how big of a pile of money is necessary (at a modest, sustainable rate of return) to replace that revenue stream?

If the rate of return you want to assume is 4 percent and you are replacing a $36,000-a-year revenue stream, it means that family needs to have $900,000 of investable assets to replace that revenue stream.

WEATHERING ACUTE BUSINESS LOSSES

If you're a business owner, especially if you're in business with a partner, it's critical to think about some of the "worst-case scenarios" that can arise when you least expect them. Consider asking yourself these tough questions and working with your financial advisor to come up with viable solutions:

- How are you going to determine the value of the business?

- Where is the funding going to come from if, in fact, you someday must buy out a partner?

- What are you going to do if one of your business partners gets a divorce and the business has to come up with capital to pay off the ex-spouse? How is that going to work?

- What if one of your partners becomes disabled and can't come to work every day, yet expects and needs the salary or profits that come from the business to survive? Where is the revenue going to come from to pay for that while you hire someone else to do the work?

- What happens if your partner dies? Do you want to accept his or her family or widowed spouse as a business partner, or are you going to have to come up with the cash to buy that interest from the estate?

The best way to hedge against all of these catastrophic losses is to pay the extra money and get disability and life insurance.

Asset protection is all about identifying what your "assets" are, what their unique value is to your situation, what the probability is of something bad happening, what the extent of damage to your financial situation would be if the worst were to happen, and finally, how the damage can be minimized, deflected, or covered by a third party.

"A true conservationist is a man who knows that the world is not given by his fathers but borrowed from his children."

—William Audubon

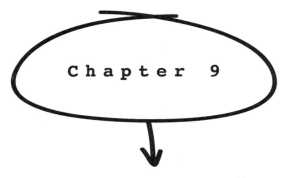

Chapter 9

Passing on the Wealth: "Who's Gonna Get the Money, Honey?"

"The unexamined life is not worth living."

—Socrates

What do you want to happen to your money after you die? I want to discuss this in two very different contexts.

Knowing when it's time to sit down with your parents and have "the talk" is never easy.

There are warning signs worth keeping an eye out for. My wife knew it was time to talk to her parents when she heard about one of her dad's golf outings. One guy couldn't see the fairway, the other was so deaf he couldn't hold a thirty-second conversation, and the third couldn't bend over to put his ball on the tee.

When you do decide to take the plunge and bring up your parents' finances, expect some resistance. On the surface, they're likely to tell you everything's fine. But are they really okay, both personally and financially? Have they thought about the potential pitfalls the future may hold?

Here are some less-than-pleasant scenarios to consider. Can your parents weather the costs of one of them moving into an assisted-living facility? What about a major surgery? Can they afford prolonged time in a nursing home? Are they getting their bills paid on time? Are they paying the insurance premiums? Are they buying multiple insurance policies they don't need? Or are they possibly giving too much money away to charities or "loaning" money to that overly needy, codependent child or sibling?

Maybe you're thinking it'll be easy to have a conversation with your parents about their finances. You just pour some coffee, ask some questions, and they'll tell you everything. Good luck with that. Chances are your parents grew up as part of the Greatest Generation, which means you're likely to get rebuffed when you start asking questions about their finances. Maybe they have reason to be cautious. Studies show that the people most likely to rip off the elderly are members of one's own family. So, if you get some pushback from Mom and Dad, maybe they're just wary of your intentions.

In counseling many seniors, I've found it's important to remember that you are often talking with people who were born shortly after the Great Depression and probably raised by very self-reliant parents. These people probably fought in a world war, served in Korea, or might even be flower children left over from the '60s.

And remember, you are still the kid. They still see themselves as the adults. Now you show up asking questions about *their* money. So just be warned, it may not go overly well because, up till now, the only time you ever talked to your folks about money was to ask them for something—gas money for a date, money for college, a loan to help you with a down payment on a house, or, if times were tough, money to bail you out of a financial jam.

So, what do you do? How do you break the ice? One approach you might consider is just to be as transparent as possible. Ask your parents, "Mom, Dad, can we talk?" Be honest and sincere. Perhaps mention something that you've noticed, like the mail piling up, or bills on the kitchen counter.

Find a good opening line, even if you have to steal one from a friend. Say you were talking to a friend who had mentioned that his parents were going through some financial difficulties and that got you thinking about them. Remember, if you come on too strong and act like you want to take over and run the show or give the impression that you can do a better job than they are doing, things aren't likely to go very well.

On the flipside, if you come off too soft or timid and ask, "Oh, how are you doing financially?" then you can expect to get a response like, "Oh, we're doing fine. Don't worry. We're okay. Everything's great ... have a cookie."

The key is to try to walk a fine line between those two extremes. Be direct and honest. Assure them that you don't want to take over or know every detail but that you are serious. You really want to understand their situation. Act like a consultant, or better yet, a financial fiduciary, and make it very clear that they're still in charge. It's their money.

They may not want your help. In fact, they may not even need it, either now or later, for any number of reasons. And again, if they say no and push back, unless you feel there is a medical or cognitive issue, back off and give them some space. When it involves cognitive or medical problems, that's a different situation, and you need medical and/or legal assistance. You may need to have a conversation with your parent's physician and/or their attorney.

HAVING THE TALK

If you're looking for ways to start a conversation with Mom or Dad about their finances, here are some potential icebreakers and conversation starters.

- Is there something that maybe I can do to help you manage all this paperwork every month? Because it looks like this is a bill that should've been paid a couple of months ago. How do you want me to help you handle this? Offer to help organize their files and decide what's important. Assist them in going through that stack of unopened mail or that pile of junk mail.

- Would you like me to do a little bit of research and get you some options regarding this dividend check that you receive a couple of times a year? Offer to help set up a direct deposit so their dividend checks go straight to the bank just like their Social Security.

- Ask if it would be better if their bills were on an auto pay so they would not have to write checks every month.

- Why don't we get on the phone together and call your investment guy and ask him a few questions about these statements that we don't seem to understand?

- Are there any parts of this insurance policy regarding your long-term care that you don't understand?

- Regarding this mutual fund that we're looking at, do you remember what initially attracted you to this investment?

- Rather than having multiple accounts with different investment companies, would it be easier if all your investments were with one organization? In other words, instead of getting six different statements, everything is reported on one.

- When it comes to your advisors, do you talk to them once a month, once a week, once a year, or once every ten years?

- Would it be easier if your advisors were local and close by, somewhere you could actually meet with them, as opposed to working with people miles away?

- How did you meet this advisor in the first place?

- Would it be okay if we went to talk to your investment advisor, insurance agent, the taxman, or the attorney together?

- What would you think of the idea of them sending me a duplicate statement, so I could get a copy of the same thing you receive? That way, if you had questions, you could ask me.

LESSONS FROM MY MOM AND DAD

I know from personal experience how difficult it can be to talk to parents about their finances. Years ago, I visited my folks in South Dakota and noticed an unopened envelope on the kitchen counter. I immediately recognized it as an annual report on a life insurance policy. Mom and Dad had never discussed their finances with me. It was always something they did on their own, so I knew I would be entering uncharted territory.

When I saw the envelope, I asked a simple question: "Hey, is this a statement on your life insurance policy?" And Dad said, "Yeah," and then he followed up with a question of his own: "Do you know anything about these policies?"

We took a look at the statement and then got out the policy. I found out he'd had it for a long time and he was considering stopping payments on it. It was his understanding the policy would continue even if he stopped paying premiums. (Actually, he had some items correct but was missing some important details.)

We discussed it a little bit. I asked a few questions. He could answer some. He couldn't answer others. So, together we called the insurance company and gathered additional information that was very helpful to him in making an appropriate decision about continuing to pay premiums.

That was a turning point for us. After that, my dad opened up. We discussed their IRA accounts. He asked me questions about these Roth accounts he'd heard so much about. After we talked and it was clear he was still in control, he elected to move some of his IRA money into a Roth.

A few years later Dad was diagnosed with cancer. After the diagnosis, I came home for a visit, and he asked me to come down with him to his room where he kept his records. He opened a file drawer and pointed to a document. "This is the will," he said. "This is the trust. This is all the information about my health insurance. Here are my past tax returns. Here's the phone number for the accountant. Here's the phone number for the lawyer. And the last file in the back of the drawer is my obituary."

At that point, I became a little uncomfortable with the conversation. But I quickly realized that it was important to Dad that we go through all this stuff *now*. I decided that if it was important to him, then I just needed to suck it up and let him explain all of this stuff to me—in his own way.

A few months later he called the local mortuary and made all the final arrangements for both his and my mom's funerals while they were still alive. He paid for them, too. So, when the time came, everything was taken care of. He and Mom made all their own decisions, with just a small amount of guidance and moral support from me. It was done the way they wanted it to be done.

He ended up living for three more very, very good years, and during that time period, we had plenty of opportunities to go through more of his stuff. When Dad passed away, we had things squared away for my mom within a few days. When she passed away six years later, my siblings and I had the entire estate settled within eleven months. Dad made it easy for my siblings and me. We will always be very grateful.

THE FINANCIAL SCAVENGER HUNT

I know, however, that Dad's case was unique. He was a very organized guy, and he wanted things to be easy for Mom and for the rest of us. He was not a procrastinator; he took action.

In other cases, elderly parents can be so disorganized that they leave their children or beneficiaries to embark on what I affectionately call "a financial scavenger hunt," which can be a real mess. Multiple bank accounts and stock certificates—sometimes in Dad's name, sometimes in Mom's, some, perhaps, with their names spelled incorrectly. You'll often find certificates from companies that no longer even exist. Some certificates in trust list both Mom and Dad as trustees even though Dad died five years ago. Some of these stock certificates have such scant value that it almost doesn't pay to mess with them.

Sometimes there are multiple life insurance policies—some still in force, some lapsed because somebody forgot to pay a premium. Some may have been canceled twenty years ago, but nobody threw them out. Oftentimes, we'll find material from an insurance company that doesn't exist anymore, because it was acquired by another company. The paperwork to organize all this is quite manageable—as long as the account owners are still alive. However, to organize finances after a person's death can easily turn into a full-time job for surviving family members.

I've seen people spend hours upon hours on the phone, attempting to get all their parents' affairs in order as they try to collect insurance policies, IRA, 401(k) plan assets, stock certificates, real estate, bank accounts, annuities, coin collections, and decades of household items. All of this is so much easier to do while people are still alive.

So, here's a quick piece of advice to the matriarchs and patriarchs in the family: if you really want to torment your kids, if they were really the teenagers from hell that caused you all kinds of grief in life, then send them on a financial scavenger hunt when you die. Give 'em hell. Hide the money.

If you've got more of a soft spot for them, though, get your affairs in order and get everything organized. Bring them into the conversation. It doesn't have to be difficult, and you don't have to give up control. Believe me. It'll make everyone's life easier.

Once again, when aging parents just aren't up to initiating these conversations, it's vital for the kids to broach the subject. Offer to help—don't take over. You might be surprised; they might actually welcome your offer to work with them. In the end, there are three words you have to remember: **coordinate**, **consolidate**, **simplify**. Make things easy for them, and you'll make things easier for yourself in the process.

AVOID THE DRAMA: TIPS ON
DIVIDING THE FAMILY ESTATE

In most families, there's one child who tends to be closer to Mom and Dad than his or her siblings. This child may be more focused on their financial affairs or maybe just lives closer—and thus, possibly by default, is more involved. It's been my experience that everybody in the family should be in the loop and be given regular updates and details on an ongoing basis.

Unfortunately, too many families split apart over finances. It's always my hope that all siblings agree that this is Mom and Dad's money and not their pending inheritance. Hopefully, the parents have laid out their wishes for the distribution of these assets upon their passing, but until they've left this planet, it's their money, and everything should be done in Mom and Dad's best interests. As their children, our jobs are to assist them just as they assisted us when we were young.

Talk to Mom and Dad. Get their feelings, and make sure any siblings are on the same page. Have a conversation with the CPA, the attorney, and the financial advisor. Remember that "talking" with Mom and Dad also has to involve listening.

DIVIDING ASSETS: EQUAL MAY NOT BE FAIR

When we began, we were talking about using your financial GPS so you could chart the right course into and through retirement. However, at some point, you will also have to acknowledge when the journey (or at least your portion of it) may be nearing an end. This is the point when hard decisions must be made. What do you want to happen to your assets? What's important to you? What do you care about? Who do you care about?

The default answer I get from most families is, "Oh. It's all going to go to the kids. We'll just divide it up and split it among the kids." Whenever I hear that response, I feel I have a responsibility to ask a difficult follow-up question: "Is the inheritance that you are going to bequeath to your children at some point in the future going to help them or hurt them?"

Think about that for a moment. Do all of your children live "normal" lives? Are they all in stable relationships? Do they all have good jobs? What are their individual family dynamics? And again, what's important to you?

Someone once pointed out to me that equal may not always be fair. What if you have three children: a son who's a surgeon, a daughter who's a corporate attorney, and a third child, the youngest, who is maybe a teacher or a social worker. Knowing that they may have very different financial profiles, you have to ask yourself, "Is equal always fair?" It's not my job to answer that question. I'm not telling you what to do, but it is something to think about.

Let me give you a hypothetical situation to ponder. Let's say that you are the head of the family business. You've run this business for fifty to sixty years, and it represents 66 percent of your net worth. One of your children, Beverly, has grown up in the business and has worked with you for thirty years. The other two kids are not involved. They don't want to be involved in the business, and they may not even get along with the heir apparent to the business who's been working for you for three decades. What are you going to do with your estate?

If that business represents 66 percent of your assets, are you going to give one child 66 percent of your net worth and let your other two children split the other 34 percent? Or do all three kids get an equal split of the business? Should the one who's worked with you for thirty years have to share the business profits every year with siblings who don't have an active role in the business? What are you going to do? Sometimes "evening up" the estate can be a challenge.

Allow me to interject a possible solution: You—the parents in our hypothetical example—take out a **second-to-die life insurance policy** that pays $900,000 when the second spouse dies. (Check with your planner to ask about details.) Your total estate is now $2,400,000 ($1M business + $500k house + $900k life insurance). Split evenly three ways that translates into $800,000 for each child. Beverly gets the business she has worked for and earned without debt. The other two split the life insurance money and sell the house. Everyone now inherits $800,000.

Everyone's financial situation is unique, and individual family dynamics are always very different. These types of decisions require you to receive input from all members of your team: the tax professional, the legal team who will draft your documents and deal with the estate after your death, and your financial planner who should know a great deal about your finances and family dynamics.

I have seen people delay decisions and the drafting of documents out of fear of getting things wrong. Bad idea. These documents are not set in concrete. They are revocable and can be amended as long as both spouses are still alive. They can even be worded in such a way that they can be amended even if one spouse has died.

My suggestion? Start the process. Get your first version completed and put in the drawer. Then commit to a periodic review. This is part of that "System 2" hard work stuff I've mentioned before. Avoidance will not help. Delay is not a solution. After you get a document completed one time, it gets easier to review and amend if necessary in the future. It's sort of like getting in the swimming pool.

It may feel cold initially. But you soon get used to it, and eventually it really does feel good.

CHARITABLE GIVING

Are there charities, organizations, colleges, churches, environmental groups, social service organizations, or homeless shelters that you care a great deal about? Would you like to share some of your wealth with them? If the answer to that question is yes, but you're unsure if you have enough money to do so, speak with your attorney, accountant, or financial advisor to explore options, because there are ways of making donations that may not necessarily disinherit your children. If you have charitable intent, explore it. Think about it. Talk about it with your heirs. Find out what's important to them. They might say, "Give it all away to charity. We don't need it."

Of course, most kids may not say that at all—but trust me when I say that sitting down and discussing things while everyone is still alive can prevent a great deal of pain later. Explain to your children what you're doing and more importantly why you are doing it. Don't leave anything to them and their siblings to try to decipher (and squabble about) when they are settling your estate. Have that conversation now. Let them in on why you're doing what you're doing.

Think about the experience that you had either with your parents or your in-laws. What worked in those situations? What didn't work? If you want to hear some horror stories, call me sometime. I can share lots of them.

Like I said, my folks were great. Everything was organized and it worked out well. However, you probably know somebody who had to go through one of those scavenger hunts. Maybe it was you. You can eliminate difficulties for your family by getting things organized. Consolidate, simplify, and organize.

Remember, none of the decisions you're making today are set in stone. This is all stuff that can be changed—providing you're still on the planet. So, don't feel that just because you've made a decision, it can't be changed. I've seen estate documents that were never changed after the initial draft because no changes were needed. However, in some larger families with more complicated dynamics and long-lived parents, ten or more amendments after the initial draft are also not unusual.

Once again, have the conversation with your children, with your attorney, with your CPA, and with your financial advisor because you will get a different perspective from each of those people. Trust me, you're going to want to hear different opinions from each of them. I've seen a lot of situations that got messed up horribly because someone only spoke with one advisor and failed to get the perspectives of others.

Paul's story is one that comes to mind. His father was an educator, a college professor. He had saved a lot of money and had named his trust as the beneficiary of all of his retirement accounts—including an annuity—because that is what the attorney suggested. At the time that Paul's dad passed away, that annuity had a $350,000 profit. Seems okay at first blush, right? Not so fast.

Paul was an only child and, therefore, the only beneficiary of the trust. Since the trust was the beneficiary of the annuity, the trust had to receive the proceeds of the annuity within five years of his dad's date of death, which also meant that Paul would have to pay taxes on that $350,000 profit within five years. During that five-year time frame, Paul was still working full time. So unfortunately for him, the $70,000 worth of profit each year for five years was added to his income and taxed at his highest tax rate.

This was an avoidable mistake. If Paul's dad had also spoken with his CPA, he would've understood this, and he may have decided to name Paul by name as the beneficiary of the annuity. Had Paul been listed by name, he would've been able to spread that profit out over his lifetime, or at least defer the bulk of it until after he had retired so the income tax burden wouldn't be so extreme.

The problem? His dad didn't talk to his tax advisor. He only talked to his attorney, whose recommendation was to name the trust. Now, in some contexts, that might have been perfectly great advice, but in this case, it ended up costing Paul a huge tax hit that possibly could've been avoided.

Remember, when you look at your assets and decide who's going to receive what, sometimes taxation makes a big difference. Sometimes your financial advisor and tax advisor may be able to put some of this in the proper context. Consider your beneficiaries. Who pays a lot of income tax? Who doesn't pay a lot? If you have a beneficiary who's in a low tax bracket, maybe he or she should get your IRA, while beneficiaries in the high tax brackets should get the Roth.

Let me give you an example of this in practice. Cindy's mom died with a $500,000 estate. Her documents, which she had drafted with her attorney, stated that she wanted $100,000 to go to her church. Her $50,000 Roth should go to her grandkids to help pay for college, and her IRA, valued at $150,000 plus the rest of the estate was to go to Cindy, who (with her husband) was in the highest tax bracket. The grandchildren who inherited the Roth were students, so they paid no income tax.

The better suggestion would have been to arrange for the charity to receive the $100,000 from the IRA account because the charity wasn't going to pay any income tax. The grandkids could have gotten the other $50,000 from the IRA because they were in a low tax bracket. Cindy could have kept all of the after-tax and Roth monies because she and her husband are in a high tax bracket. In cases like these, there is almost always a better solution—it just takes some planning to find what it is.

THE CHOICE IS *YOURS*.

In the end, it's all about finding out what's important to you. What do you want to do? There shouldn't be any regrets. Eventually we all get to a point in time where you can't do it over again. You need to really think about what's important. What do you want to do? What's your legacy? What's your philosophy?

It's not about how you want to be remembered. It's more about how you want to live—and what kind of difference you want to make. That being said, some people don't care about making a difference, and that's fine. No judgment here. It's just that I find some of the happiest people in life are the ones who have thought about these very difficult issues.

I offer up my mom and my dad again as prime examples. Late in their lives, I don't think either one of them had any regrets—nothing they wish they had done. It wasn't that they did everything; it was more that they had become comfortable with where they were and who they were. They realized that they had lived a good, satisfying life.

I sincerely hope that this book, in some greater or lesser way, helps provide you with the very same comfort and satisfaction in your own lives, no matter where along the journey you may be now, or where you are planning to go in the future.

CONCLUSION

I know the phrase "no regrets" gets a lot of play in music. Always has. Probably always will. Tom Rush. Waylon Jennings. Emmylou Harris. They all croon about regret, because regret is one of the most powerful forces in our lives.

Far too often, a great deal of energy is expended on past decisions. People beat themselves up, blame others, blame circumstance, blame God. Maybe it's not anyone's fault. Perhaps it is just bad luck. Wrong place, wrong time. Stuff happens.

I think we're all best served by occasionally looking at our lives and asking ourselves some tough questions: Do I have regrets? Is this regret helping or hurting my life now? Should I "get over it" and move on? What are my priorities? What are the things, without exception, that I really want to see happen? If I cannot have it all, what is "really not that important to me" if I have to give something up to make my priorities a reality?

The truth of the matter is that one's financial life—and life in general—is really not about keeping score. Then again, if we're being real here, we have to admit that most people, whether consciously or subconsciously, do keep score—just like my four-year-old grandson in peewee soccer.

It's important to reflect on your life—and to do it for the rest of your life. Try to get beyond the regrets. Are there things you wanted to do that you still haven't been able to do? If so, laying them out on the table is the first step toward trying to achieve them.

Looking forward, where are your priorities? What's really important to you? What do you really need to have happen? Then again, what's not so important? This book has been a testament to the power of coming to grips with your financial reality and matching that reality with the narrative playing out in your head.

We've talked a lot about those special two blue dots: where you currently are on your financial GPS, and where you want to go. There's nothing you can do about all those blue dots from your past—all the places you've been and choices you've already made—but there is plenty you can do in charting the best course forward.

There's no judgment involved in any of this. If you want to travel more, if you want to continue to live in the big house, if you want to fund the education of your grandchildren, or embark on a major trip around the world, or build that master suite you've dreamed about for years, go for it. It might require you working another five or ten or even fifteen years—or doing less later in life. You just need to know your options so you can make decisions. As I've mentioned before, there are no bad decisions as long as you've made the decisions for the right reasons.

Consider this. I saw a cartoon not too long ago. It showed two people sitting in the front seat of a car. The driver was getting ready to program his GPS. The gentleman in the passenger seat had a shaved head, was wearing a robe, and was obviously a monk. He looked at the driver who was getting ready to program the GPS and offered a little pearl of wisdom: "Program the journey," the monk said, "not the destination."

There's a lot of wisdom stenciled into that cartoon. It reminded me of a gentleman who came into my office for a consultation one day. I asked, as I always do, about his priorities in life, his financial goals, and what he wanted out of life. "I only have one goal," he said. "I want to make sure the check to the undertaker bounces." Translation: he wanted to spend all his money, have a good time, and die broke.

We laughed about it. I thought it was a funny joke. But over the years, I began to realize his goals were not that simple. There were many things he cared deeply about. He wanted to know his options, think about his alternatives, and enjoy the pleasures of his life, which included family and charities.

This book has been about looking carefully at the two blue dots that are guiding your future. We all need to recognize that the second blue dot, in reality, is the destination. So take a deep breath and enjoy the journey.

Thank you for spending your time to read this book. I hope these pages have given you food for thought and will assist you on your financial journey through life. I welcome your comments and feedback on what you have read. Feel free to call or email me; you can find my contact information in the back of this book.

—Fred

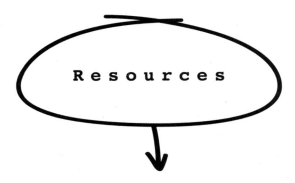

Resources

Clark, David. *The Tao of Charlie Munger*. Scribner, 2017.

Fox, Justin. *The Myth of the Rational Market*. Harper Business, 2009.

Gladwell, Malcolm. *Blink*. Back Bay Books, Little, Brown, 2005.

Goldie, Daniel, and Gordon Murray. *The Investment Answer*. Grand Central Publishing, 2011.

Kahneman, Daniel. *Thinking Fast and Slow*. Farrar, Straus and Giroux, 2011.

Lewis, Michael. *The Undoing Project*. Norton, 2017.

Murray, Nicholas. *Simple Wealth, Inevitable Wealth*. The Nick Murray Company, 2013.

Pompian, Michael. *Behavioral Finance and Wealth Management*. Wiley, 2012.

Richards, Carl. *The Behavior Gap*. Portfolio/Penguin, 2012.

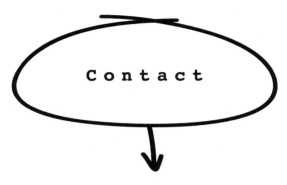

To learn more about the various services that my team and I offer and for more information on how I may assist you, visit my website at **www.fredwollman.com**.

Email: **info@fredwollman.com**

Phone: **760-737-2246**